Memories of Merritt Island

BIRTHPLACE OF KENNEDY SPACE CENTER

Best Wishes to Norman

by Gail Briggs Nolen

Gail Briggs Nolen

Library of Congress Number: 2004107068
ISBN 0-9753023-1-0

AMMONS COMMUNICATIONS
29 Regal Avenue • Sylva, North Carolina 28779
Phone/fax: (828) 631-4587

Note: The information contained in this book is not necessarily in chronological order. Every attempt was made to correctly identify each person. The photos are from family collections unless otherwise noted.

Dedication

To my husband Joe for his guidance, love, understanding, support, patience and editing skills. Thank you!

Andy & Teresa Nolen,
Tracy & Chris Nolen,
Gail & Joe Nolen
Our grand dogs left to right:
Latté, Chevas (the Cocker Spaniel),
Stella (in chair) and Dee

To my sons, Chris and Andy, who are fifth generation Benecke's in America and tenth generation Briggs' in America.

To my three 'crazy' cousins from Florida: Anna Laura, Evelyn, and Iris; to my cousin Ray, his brother June Benecke and their wives Catherine and Audrey who have trusted me with family items, pictures, memorabilia, advice, and information. I also thank you for allowing me into your home, lives and hearts.

A special thank you to my good friend and author, Amy Ammons Garza, for her encouragement and belief in me.

And to Fran, Polly and Serena, writer friends forever!

Acknowledgements

What a joy and pleasure it has been to see my family's history come alive through the stories and pictures that have been shared in the gathering of information for this book. The many hours spent getting reacquainted with cousins, aunts, and uncles have been heartwarming, creating enduring memories for me.

To all who have contributed, I thank you from the bottom of my heart for helping me share our rich family history with others.

The history of our family on Merritt Island is unique, yet at the same time common to all the pioneering families who lived there. This book is an attempt to forever capture memories of life on the island that will pass away with my generation. Having to move off Merritt Island was traumatic for many families. Perhaps by reliving those memories, some healing can take place.

In one of his lectures, Merritt Island author Patrick Smith explains that everyone needs what he calls a sense of place; a place where they belong, where they come from, where they feel comfortable, a place they call home.

To many of the members of my family their sense of place is North Merritt Island, where their parents and grandparents homesteaded and where they grew up.

Even though it has been over forty years since they were uprooted during the land acquisition to enlarge the Kennedy Space Center, they still feel tied to the land around Happy Creek.

2004

Mouth of Happy Creek

Forward

"I believe that this nation should commit itself to achieving the goal, before this decade is out, of landing a man on the moon and returning him safely to earth. No single space project in this period will be more exciting or more impressive to mankind or more important for the long-range exploration of space and none will be so difficult or expensive to accomplish . . . . In a very real sense, it will not be one man going to the moon –it will be an entire nation. For all of us must work together to put him there."

President John F. Kennedy
Congress, May 25, 1961

Our president's challenge put many wheels into motion in 1961. One step in building a spaceport was finding a location. North Merritt Island was chosen, in part, because of the Air Force influence at Cape Canaveral. In the process, NASA had to work out an understanding with the Air Force that would secure freedom of action in NASA's launch area.

Before recommending any purchase of land, the dangers involved in testing and launching a moon vehicle had to be determined. Although there had been a missile test site in the area for many years, additional safety precautions would be needed. The hazards in a project like this required a secured distance between the launch pad and uncontrolled areas. The board assigned to study this project concluded that if the government acquired additional land on Merritt Island, rockets could be launched from onshore facilities along False Cape north of Cape Canaveral. Since people working within government-controlled areas such as the Air Force Base could be given adequate protection, Merritt Island provided perfect locations for industrial and technical support areas.

This book is centered around that additional land purchase on Merritt Island. Both sets of my great-grandparents, the Briggs and the Beneckes, homesteaded on key portions of land which the federal government intended to acquire. The Briggs homestead was located near where the Vehicle Assembly Building (VAB) now stands. The Beneckes were located close to the present site of Launch Pad 39B.

I believe mankind has benefited from the space program. Had NASA not taken over this area that our families loved so much, North Merritt Island might have become another 'condo city.'

Now, much of it is Merritt Island National Wildlife Refuge and is as wild as it was when Carolina and Henry Benecke, my great grandmother and grandfather, saw it for the first time in the late 1880's. We are very fortunate to be able to claim this as our family's original land.

My family, along with the hundreds of other displaced persons, had their lives interrupted, many suffering lasting emotional scars. They were hurt and disappointed to find that, after all the years of living in their personal paradise on earth, it would be, as one family member said, "snatched out from under us." Understandably, they were very upset. My great-grandfather's son Herman Benecke who, like many others, thought he would never have to leave his home, died shortly after being forced to move from his beloved Merritt Island.

The first public announcement of the land acquisition came August 1961 during a local evening television newscast. My Great Aunt Anna Benecke Stalder was startled to learn that her home and that of her neighbors would have to be sold. Aunt Anna communicated her feelings well in a letter to her niece, Anna Laura, dated September 1, 1961:

"Well we will have to vacate our homes before very long as the government is going to take all our homes on North Merritt Island and we don't know where we will eventually land. So far we have not found anything suitable – too much money or the land can't be bought. The Briggs' and Benecke's all have to move – no one has any choice. It is a shame. Who would have thought that we all would come to that!

I sure will hate to leave this dear old home and the grove. This spring we had a lot of work done on the house and it looks so nice, now we have to leave it. I am hoping and praying that the deal yet might fall through. Johnny (son, Johnny Stalder) will loose his shop building too; his tools and machinery he can move. When this thing flashed on the TV, it made me sick for a week - and the boys too. Every chance we have, we go place (house) hunting. As yet we have not found anything suitable made.

Your loving Aunt Anna"

Johnny Stalder's machine shop

The announcement, also heralded in the Titusville Star-Advocate newspaper, stated that land on North Merritt Island would be purchased from its current owners via land acquisition by the U.S. Government for the purpose of space exploration. This announcement came as a complete surprise to some landowners; no government official had yet contacted them.

During 1961, an agent of the government offered one of my cousins $27,000 for his home and fish camp, which included over 33 acres. He was told there was some leeway and the offer could go as high as $34,500. Since the property had recently been appraised at around $70,000, my cousin refused this offer and sued the government. The next year, a U.S. Marshall showed up at his home and told him that he and his family had to move within the next ten days or the government would come move them. He and his family were forced to move and did not, as others had, receive any money for his property until the trial was over five years later.

An article from the front page of the Friday, August 25, 1961 Titusville Star-Advocate read:

WE'RE NOW SPACEPORT USA
80,000 Acres Will Be Taken

Titusville became Spaceport, U.S.A. yesterday. From now on Titusville will be known as "space exploration headquarters." It will strictly be known as "moon or space land" because it is from the tract of land east of Titusville that the United States will fire its hopes toward the moon, toward Mars and into outer space.

Included in the acquisition was the town of Orsino, all of Titusville Beach, Canaveral, Sunrise, Jaycee and Playalinda Beaches, the town of Wilson, all land south of the Haulover Canal (not to be confused with present day Haulover Canal). It includes such historical points as Dummett Grove and plantation, and the old Canaveral Club. It includes many hundreds of acres of rich Indian River citrus groves. It will include many home-

steads rich in lore, history and sentiment by those who homesteaded or their heirs.

A Miami Herald article written on the subject of land acquisition stated it was a sparsely inhabited area with only 300 families living there. As this book will no doubt show you, these families loved their land. They persisted in literally hacking out a small portion of land for themselves and their families among the palmetto swamps, the thousands of mosquitoes, wild pigs, alligators, snakes, panthers, bears and bobcats. These wonderful, caring people knew only that they were losing what they had worked for all of their lives. Families on Merritt Island had developed a great deal of compassion for each other. How could they understand that this would be for the good of all? Their selfless devotion to the land, groves, farms, churches, communities and homes they lovingly built was to be no more.

With the passing of time came changes to the lives of the displaced; changes in lifestyles, jobs, dreams, health, and expectations. Join me now on a journey to Merritt Island, once a family paradise.

2004

*View of Launch Pad 39B
from former Benecke property*

2004

*View across Banana Creek of VAB
from former Futch's Landing*

*HENRY JOHAN BENECKE
CAROLINA KOELLING

    Anna   c. James Amerson, Charles Stalder, Johnny Stalder
    Lillie   c. Alice, William, Stuart, Juanette, Iris, David
    Herman Johan   c. Henry, Ray, June, Betty
    Lena   c. Evart, Leslie, Floyd, Lloyd, Harvey, Evelyn, Leland
    Laura   c. Margarette, Herman, Denton, Violette Carolyn
    Rose   c. Anna Laura, Daniel

*ELMER EZRA BRIGGS
HARRIET JERU

    Dorr
    Alta
    Nina
    Clio
    Davey
    Lila

DORR ANGELO BRIGGS
LENA CHARLOTTE BENECKE

    Evart Elmer
    Leslie
    Floyd
    Lloyd
    Harvey
    Evelyn Harriet
    Leland

My Family Chart

EVART ELMER BRIGGS
GLADYS ROBERTSON

    Shirley Yvonne
    Celia
    Gail
    Barbara
    Leslie Dorr

JOSEPH EDWARD NOLEN
GAIL BRIGGS

    Christopher Edward
    Robert Andrew

*Homesteaded on Merritt Island

Henry (Henri) Johan Benecke was born in Aachen, Germany on November 19, 1863. He arrived in New York on June 19, 1882 aboard the passenger ship General Werder that sailed from Bremen, Germany (per records of the District of New York, Port of New York).

Carolina Friederika Koelling Benecke was born in Mollenbeck, Germany on December 27, 1862. It is believed that she arrived in New York also from Bremen, Germany in 1883. She was working for a wealthy family (the Hillmans) as a seamstress and they paid her way to New York.

Engagement picture, circa 1888

This baptismal record of Carolina was discovered among old German family documents.

"Extract from the baptismal register of the Reformed Parish of Mollenbeck in the county of Rinteln, province of Hessen-Nassau; Kingdom of Prussia.

In the parish of Moellenbeck, county court Rinteln, House Number 54, was born on the 27th of December 1862 (27 Dec 1862) and baptized on 7 Jan 1863:

Carolina Friederika Koelling,

legitimate daughter of the shoemaker Karl Heinrich Koelling and his wife Charlotte Hennriette, maiden name Wolter.

The godparent was Caroline Wilhelmina Henriette Pflueger from #13 in Hessendorf.

(The authenticity of this extract is certified with signature and church seal)

Mollenbeck, 17 Aug 1884   by Pastor Ratz

Carolina's home in Mollenbeck, Germany

*Karl Heinrich Koelling and Carolina
in front of family home in Germany*

Karl Heinrich Koelling
Carolina Koelling Benecke's father

Karl Heinrich Koelling
and friends in Germany

13

Grandpa Henry Benecke in sailboat

Herman Benecke learned to build boats from his father (pictured above).
By age six, Herman had his first sailboat.

Daughter-in-law Dora Benecke recorded that Henry Johan often spoke of a large home in Germany that housed several related families: "Henry was one son among four girls. He had a well rounded education that included an excellent background in music, as well as knowledge of carpentry. This knowledge was later to be a mainstay as he embarked on his life in the United States."

After finishing university in Germany, Henry did not want to serve his compulsory time in the German Army. Family stories indicate that before leaving for the United States, Henry Benecke gave up his right to the family inheritance and home in Germany to his older sister and her husband. He booked passage to America, arriving in New York City in 1882.

While in New York he became friends with a fellow German, Alphonse Hoeck. Alphonse told Henry about the abundant wilderness in a place called Florida, where his brother had homesteaded. During a Christmas holiday, the two friends traveled by train, steamship, and sailboat to visit Alphonse's brother Max. Max had established his homestead about seven miles from Dummitt Grove located on North Merritt Island. On his plot of land, Max had built a home, planted several orange groves, and was also raising bees.

After viewing the Happy Creek area of Merritt Island, Henry knew this was to be his new home. He built a small sailboat and started a new life in this exotic land for himself and his future bride. While living on the small boat tied up in Happy Creek, Henry hacked through the dense brush and palmettos, clearing enough land to satisfy the stipulations in the Homestead Act. Each day's labor was made that much more difficult by the sweltering heat, the swarms of mosquitoes and other bugs, and by the constant awareness of poisonous snakes in the surrounding thickets. Henry staked out the four corners of his homestead to include 160 acres, completed the necessary homestead papers at the county courthouse in Titusville, and sent them to Washington, D.C.

On February 13, 1888 Henry Benecke wrote the following letter to Carolina (Lina). It has been translated from old German script.

Banana River, Fla., 13 Feb. 1888

My most dearly beloved only Lina!

Finally, today on Thursday, I have received your deeply longed for letters. I was in Titusville one time, and expected to receive a letter from sweet dear, but to no avail; I stayed there another day, since I thought I would surely receive the longed-for article; but again for naught. That was on Thursday, the 2nd. The following day I drove down to Mr. Quarterman's grove, where I am now. I am fixing up his somewhat neglected place and receive half of the fruit in return. I have a good house here. I think that we could live here happily and contentedly. My most dearly beloved Lina, I cannot offer you more than a very simple life.

But, as I know my Lina, I believe that happiness and contentment shall never depart from our door step. And we have true and faithful neighbors and friends here; our closest neighbor, whose house is only 200 to 300 paces from ours, is Mr. Orlando Quarterman's brother George, with his

wife and three children. They're wonderful people. My only wish is this, for my Lina to be here now. Oh, what a happy time it would be for us! Many people think, perhaps, that in such an out-of-the-way area people are extremely ignorant and without education. But that is not at all true. The people here are neither highly educated nor ignorant, yet they are smarter than Northerners under similar circumstances.

Now, my heart's Lina, don't think that I believe you are neglecting your Henry. Oh no my sweet Lina, I know you better than that. I do know how much you love me; that your fondest thoughts are of me alone.

I would have received your letters sooner if I had been able to go to the post office. However, you must remember that I am now 16 miles from Heath and about 30 miles from Titusville. Here we belong to the post office of Canaveral. However, I had not said anything to the post master in Titusville as to where I wanted my mail to go, because I also did not know how long I would stay here; if I wouldn't be coming back to Titusville again in a few days. However, I had so much work that I had no time to drive around. Also, I will stay here another week and plant more vegetables. Then I have to look for work for a month or two and earn some money.

Now is the time when many birds wear plumes; then they are extremely shy so that it is very difficult to get them within a shot's reach. Soon I will go out in my boat for several days and hunt; perhaps I can send a dozen or so. Right now it is still a little bit too early. When I was on my way to Titusville a few days ago, I heard the quacking of ducks in a nearby pond. I landed, snuck up close and found so many ducks that they were almost sitting on top of each other.

Unfortunately both barrels of my gun failed; otherwise, I believe, I would have hit fifty of them with those two shots; ducks are now bringing in fifteen cents apiece. If Mr. Hillman wants to pay the costs, I will send him a dozen as soon as I have the opportunity. I am glad that the oranges have arrived; hopefully in good condition. Tell me, my Lina, my heart's Lina, who sent the three dollars? You or the Hillmans; please tell me the truth. Tell Mr. Hillman that I do not smoke. I do not drink and do not smoke either.

Now, my heart's Lina, I don't want to say anymore about the Hillmans. Most of all I do not wish to sadden you, my dearly beloved, sweet Lina, at any cost. Lina, I ask you so very much that when sometimes I become hard and rough you will forgive me and remember that faithfulness and honesty rest beneath all this roughness. It is impossible for me to present a smooth and polished appearance. Also, I know quite well that Lina, if she recognized me to be a pretender, would despise me. A liar and a thief are most miserable among all the people. Thank God that the two have not yet pushed forward into our area. There is a man here who is thought by everyone to be a scoundrel, even though nobody can prove anything against him; I will tell you his name since one can never know what it might be good for. His name is F.B. Sachet; he is the post master at Heath.

Now I would also like to ask you, my only beloved Lina, to also be a little careful. What pains you must have suffered here with a burnt arm! And remember Lina, when you are suffering, I also suffer with you. A year ago I would have been happy to meet a panther or a bear, armed only with a knife, and I threw myself into the waves with my boat in a daredevil manner. Then, I would not have thought anything of it. But now, my dear Lina, I am your property, your life. My soul now belongs to you. Now I am more careful. Whereas formerly my life was without goal, now I have holy obligations. My Lina, I hardly think that my sister will ever visit you. At least she has enough other entertainment. I don't hear anything from the other two. Marie and Meta, they also don't have any time to send their brother a few lines.

Oh Lina! I feel compelled with all force to call out: "Lina, my Lina, come to me! Tell me, my Lina, what is holding you back?" You said that you are not afraid to travel alone. Also, there is no reason to be afraid, because in the wintertime so many guests come down. If it didn't cost so much, I wouldn't be waiting very long to get you. But this way it can hardly work out.

Lina, tell me do you want to give me your hand in that eternal bond around Christmas? Do you want to speak your vow with me in front of the pastor in Titusville then? Oh Lina, surely it will seem to you as though I am asking too much of you, but you will recognize yourself that it wouldn't only be my greatest happiness, but that for you, my dear heart, this is also best.

If you love me in the way my heart tells me, and you have told me, oh!, then you will know no better place than next to my heart, at the side of him who loves you above everything and whose only purpose is to make you happy.

Now, I think I will have to end for this time and close this letter. Please my dear Lina, write back right away. The clock shows past ten o'clock. I have been writing for nearly three hours. Now, good night my heart. Dream of. . your Henry"

Written on back of last page:

Mr. Henry Benecke
Narrows
c/o Dredge Chester, Florida

Please also send me one or two pencils

18

Grandpa Benecke's Petition for Citizenship, sworn to on November 12, 1894.

He filed on September 18, 1887 stating that he had resided in America since July 2, 1882.

In County Court
Brevard County, Florida

In the matter of
The Petition of Henry Benecke
to become a Citizen

To the Hon Minor S. Jones, Judge of said Court.
The Petition of Henry Benicke sheweth to the Court —
(1) That Petitioner on the 28th day of September 1887 filed in the Clerk's Office for the County of Brevard, State of Florida his declaration under oath of his intention to become a Citizen of the United States of America, and to renounce forever all allegiance and fidelity to every foreign prince potentate state and sovereignty whatsoever; and particularly to William 2nd King of Prussia and Emperor of Germany of whom he is a subject.
(2) That your petitioners has resided in the United States for over twelve years, to wit from the 2nd of July 1882 to the present time without ever having been out of the same for that period.
(3) Petitioner further shews that he is over 21 years of age.
Your petitioner therefore prays that he be admitted to take the oath of fealty and allegiance to the United States of America, and to be declared a citizen of the same.

Henry Benecke

4—772.

The United States of America,

TO ALL TO WHOM THESE PRESENTS SHALL COME, GREETING:

Homestead Certificate No. *11650*

Application *18215*

Whereas there has been deposited in the GENERAL LAND OFFICE of the United States a CERTIFICATE of the Register of the Land Office at *Gainesville Florida*, whereby it appears that, pursuant to the Act of Congress approved 20th May, 1862, "To secure Homesteads to actual settlers on the public domain," and the acts supplemental thereto, the claim of *Henry Benecke* has been established and duly consummated in conformity to law for the *West half of the North East quarter, the North West quarter of the South East quarter and the North East quarter of the South West quarter of section thirty-one in Township twenty one South of Range thirty-seven East of Tallahassee Meridian in Florida containing one hundred and sixty acres*

according to the Official Plat of the Survey of the said Land returned to the GENERAL LAND OFFICE by the SURVEYOR GENERAL.

Now know ye, That there is therefore granted by the UNITED STATES unto the said *Henry Benecke* the tract of Land above described: TO HAVE AND TO HOLD the said tract of Land, with the appurtenances thereof, unto the said *Henry Benecke* and to *his* heirs and assigns forever.

In testimony whereof, I, *Grover Cleveland* President of the United States of America, have caused these letters to be made Patent, and the Seal of the General Land Office to be hereunto affixed.

Given under my hand, at the City of Washington, the *ninth* day of *October*, in the year of Our Lord one thousand eight hundred and *ninety five*, and of the Independence of the United States the one hundred and *twentieth*.

By the President: *Grover Cleveland*

By *M*. *Mc Kean* Sec'y.

L. S.

A. C. Lamar, Recorder of the General Land Office.

Henry was granted 160 acres of land on October 19, 1895 under the 1862 Homestead Act.

Henry and Carolina Benecke's Home

Banana Creek – looking north

The home of Lena and Dorr Briggs

"East side of our home on Merritt Island; the house that burned down. Daddy (Dorr Briggs) built the dragline that dug the ditch around the four acres of land," Evelyn Briggs Smith. Evelyn remembers the day this house burned.

Mr. Henry Heinlien – after the hunt

24

Early photo of a Happy Creek camp

Henry and Carolina raised six happy children on Merritt Island. Pictured above are Herman, Lena, Anna, Laura and Lillie.

Rose, the youngest, was born two years later. Anna is wearing a hat made from palmetto palm leaves. Carolina, a seamstress, made all the clothes for her family.

Lillie, Herman, Lena and Rose outside the back of the kitchen; Anna is just inside the door. Having caught enough trout in Banana Creek one year, Henry was able to add this kitchen.

View of the kitchen of Henry Johan Benecke home—
Kitchens were built separate from the main house due to the heat and possible fire hazard.
Notice the barrel at left, used to catch rainwater for cooking.

Dorr Briggs and Herman Benecke after a successful hunt on Merritt Island

Herman Benecke and his dog

The Henry Johan Benecke family home

Henry and Carolina hunted and fished the lands and waters around their primitive home. Henry worked as a carpenter and a gunsmith. Carolina made the sails for the boat Henry made. They taught music to their six children, and Henry made a zither which is now in my possession.

The family home was often alive with music during the evenings, blending with the neighboring sounds of panthers, bears, wildcats, and gators. Each child was taught respect and love for the outdoors and for each other.

Pictured from left to right are: Herman, unidentified, Rose, Anna, Lillie, Lena, and Laura.

Front row: Lena, Lillie, Laura
Back row: Anna, Carolina, Rose, Henry, Herman

My great-grandfather, Henry Johan is at the back left.
The other men are unidentified.

33

Herman Benecke
Photo taken for enlistment in World War II

Captain Benecke (Herman)
with his ducks

34

Mr. George Gurkey, a professional photographer from the Boston area, pictured above, visited Happy Creek Hunting and Fishing Camp in the early 1900's.

He took many pictures of the Happy Creek area, some of which are featured on the following pages. This was the first time the camera had been used for a private "shoot."

A cabin on Merritt Island

Mr. George Gurkey with a bobcat.

The Henry Benecke home on Happy Creek

The Little Creek
by Rose Benecke Deneff

"I wandered up and down the little creek where I used to play when I was a little girl – way out on the east coast of Florida. Down by the little creek there stands the house where the old folks used to live and I wandered and played as a child.
I sailed, rowed and motored by boat up and down the little creek by day and by night."

My Childhood Days

This was found among Lillie Benecke Caudill's papers after she died. It is believed to have been written by her sister Rose who was the youngest of the six children and still living at home when her mother Carolina died.

The year of 1911, my mother died. I was a child of 11. My older sisters and brother married and left home. I was left with my father and stepmother.

Rose is under the protective arm of her father.

My parents had six children – four sisters and one brother, all older than myself. They were all healthy children except myself. I seemed to be ailing from the time I was born until I was fourteen years of age. Mother and father would sit by my bedside and hold my hand to keep me quiet and try to ease my pain. My brother and sisters would play with me during the daytime until I was old enough to go places with them. Then they would slip off from me, as I could not play like they did, so I had to learn to play all alone most of the time.

There was a little stream that ran through our garden. Father built a triphammer for us children to play with but I could not play in fresh water so I had to stand on the bank and watch the rest play.

One day they missed me. I was about three years old, so everyone was looking all over the place. Finally everyone decided that I may have gone down to the creek and sure enough, I had and had fell in and swam halfway across which was about a quarter of a mile wide. One of my sisters came in a boat and rescued me. That experience did not hurt me so I was allowed to play in the creek from then on, as it was salt water. I learned to swim, float, turn somersaults in the water and to swim underwater like a fish or like an alligator which were plentiful in those days.

We children would go in swimming but

39

before we did we would sit on the dock and watch for the alligators, and when they raised their heads out of the water, we would call Father to come and shoot them. He usually got one.

Our parents had a private teacher for the older children for several years. When I was four in the fall of 1904, I started the first grade. January, when I became five, I finished my first grade during the term. We did not have a teacher for several seasons. It was about 1907 before we got another teacher and I finished the second grade. Then we had no more school until 1913.

My mother died in May 1911. That left me a very lonely child. Father married again in 1913. That same year there was another school two miles away. I had to walk there every morning and back every evening through water, mud, grass and brush where there were plenty of snakes, some bear, panthers, skunks and what not. That year I skipped the third and fourth grade and finished the fifth.

The following year I finished the sixth and started the seventh which I never finished although if I had and gone thru a summer school, I could have taught school the following fall; but for various reasons I didn't!

Note: A school teacher would not come to Merritt Island unless there were at least three students to teach.

Written on the top of photo: *"This old homestead where Kennedy Space Center is now. Kitchen in background."*

This was a post card sent to "Miss Laura Benecke" with the following note:

"Dear sister Laura, Here is a picture that I took. What do you think of it? I developed or rather printed over the…..(illegible). This is Ma and Rose."

The people of North and South Merritt Island built a bridge (pictured above) across the Banana Creek. They built it tall enough to accommodate the Widgeon, a large supply boat. The local residents named this bridge the Humpback Bridge.

The bridge was replaced around 1937. In its place now is NASA's shuttle crawlway. My paternal grandfather Dorr Briggs helped erect the first two bridges.

Information supplied by Ray Benecke. Picture courtesy of Evelyn Briggs Smith, taken November, 1945

My father Evart and his brother Leslie Briggs with alligator.
'Alligator Lena' was their mother, pictured on next page.

This is Lena Benecke Briggs with an alligator she caught on the Briggs Homestead. She earned the nickname 'Alligator Lena' by catching alligators to sell to tourists who would come to the fishing and hunting camps in the area.

When he was ten years old in 1904, Herman and his sister Anna were out in their rowboat when they were attacked by an alligator. The gator bit a chunk out of the rowboat. Herman shot the gator, but had to go back later and kill it so it would not attack anyone else.

Evelyn Briggs Smith in one of the alligator nests that populated Merritt Island during the 1920's.

L-R: Herman Benecke, Dorr Briggs, the preacher (unidentified), Lena Benecke and Lila Briggs at the wedding of Dorr and Lena on December 21, 1913.

Lena and Dorr raised seven children: Evart (my father), Leslie, twins Floyd and Lloyd (Lloyd died at age 5), Harvey, Evelyn and Leland.

Evelyn remembers her mother saying, *"We married under a camphor tree on the island."*

The two youngest children of Lena and Dorr are still living and both are on the east coast of Florida. Evelyn is living in Cocoa; Leland lives in Port Orange, near Daytona.

First row: Leslie, Floyd, Lloyd, Evart Briggs
Second row: Lena, holding Harvey, Dorr Briggs

Floyd Briggs, Daniel Deneff, Rose Benecke Deneff, Anna Laura Deneff, Lena Benecke Briggs, Harvey Briggs, John Deneff. Leland Briggs is standing next to his mother, Lena.

Laura Benecke Koleff with her husband, Pete and daughter Margarette in 1918

Anna Benecke Stalder with her son Charlie

Herman and Margarett Koleff were all dressed up for this picture.

Herman is holding an American flag. These were the two oldest of four children of Laura and Pete Koleff.

Herman George was born on August 24, 1919; Margarette Rose was born on May 4, 1918

Her children identified by her own hand, Laura sent this picture to her sister, Rose, promising to paint a protrait of the children in the near future. Laura didn't get the chance to do this; she passed away at age 37.

Laura Benecke

Laura, the fifth child of Henry and Carolina Benecke was born in 1898. Laura was a skilled artist in painting and sketching portraits. Because of the health problems of her husband, she also crocheted many items, selling her work to help support her family.

Laura's husband, Pete Koleff, went blind in 1924 when their four children were still young. In 1925, having no other choice, Laura had to place the children, Margarette, Herman, Denton and Violette, in the Methodist Children's Home in Enterprise, Florida. Pete was placed in a home for the blind in Sanford, Florida where he later died.

Laura met and married Joseph LaRoche whose family was from Georgia. At this time the children returned to live with their mother and stepfather.

On July 31, 1936, Laura, at the age of 37, was tragically struck down with cervical cancer. Violette returned to the Methodist Children's Home. Margarette, Herman and Denton began life on their own.

Information supplied by Violette Carolyn Koleff Hunter Guth, daughter of Laura.

Laura is sitting in a wicker chair on this windy day. To Laura's right is a hound dog, sniffing the air.

Written on the back of this photo: "Laura Benecke (mother) 1915. Probably taken in Titusville on the old Homestead."

John & Rose, daughter Anna Laura, son Daniel

Wedding day March 1, 1919

Daniel

During World War II, Daniel F. Deneff saved a shipmate from drowning when the rubber boat they were in overturned. His friend Johnny Chervnko had torn a ligament in his leg and was unable to swim. Daniel kept him afloat until another shipmate (unnamed) helped him pull Johnny safely to shore.

Standing in the apiary are Henry Johan, Anna, Carolina, Lena, Laura, Lillie, and Rose Benecke

Apiary on Merritt Island

This picture was taken on the Benecke homestead.
Rose Benecke is pictured on the left; the other girl is unidentified.

Laura Benecke

Rose Benecke

Johnny Stalder, his mother Anna, and her sister Lillie, Chester Shoals Coast Guard Station on Merritt Island.

Anna and Lillie, Chester Shoals Coast Guard Station on Merritt Island.

58

Lena Charlotte Benecke Briggs

Lena and Dorr A. Briggs' only daughter, Evelyn Briggs Smith. To her right is my oldest sister, Shirley Yvonne Briggs.

Dorr Angelo Briggs, my paternal grandfather

His nephew Ray Benecke states "A finer man you could not meet."
The article on the next page relates to Dorr's untimely death.

Briggs Funeral Services To Be Held Here Today

Funeral services for Dorr Angelo Briggs, 62, a resident of this area for 40 years, will be held at 3 p. m. today at Koon-Smith Funeral Chapel.

Briggs died from injuries suffered while he was bulldozing an area on Merritt Island. He was clearing some land Thursday for George Jacobsen when a palmetto tree broke off and fell over him, causing internal injuries in the chest and stomach. He was rushed to Wuesthoff Hospital, where he died Friday.

He was born in Evart, Michigan, Dec. 3, 1891, and came to Florida to live on property by his father on Merritt Island. He was a member of the Orsino Baptist church and had been an active religious worker for many years.

He is survived by his wife, Lena; four sons, Evart Briggs and Leland Briggs of Lakeland, Floyd K. Briggs and Harvey E. Briggs of Orsino; one daughter, Mrs. Evelyn Smith of Merritt Island; his mother, Mrs. Harriet J. Briggs of Daytona Beach; one brother, D. J. Briggs of Detroit, Michigan; four sisters, Miss Cleo Briggs and Mrs. Calvin Davis of Daytona Beach, Mrs. Gus Speigel of Owasso, Michigan, and Miss Nina O. Briggs, a former missionary in Africa but now of Pahokee.

Services today will be in charge of Rev. W. S. Singletary and Rev. James H. Christie.

Active pallbearers will be George Jacobsen, Edwin Mc-Quarters, Walter Burgess, James Garnet, George Honaker and P. L. Hightower.

Honorary pallbearers will be Frank Marion, Robert Honaker, J. O. Berry, Garnet Taylor, Rev. T. U. Fann and George Caldwell.

Interment will be in the family plot in Memorial Park Cemetery.

The Briggs'
By Ray Benecke

If you haven't been on a Benecke – Briggs Coot Shoot, you don't have any bragging rights at all. Once a year around Thanksgiving either H. J. Benecke or D. A. Briggs would suggest a picnic at Moores Creek, a strand of salt water creeks on the east side of Indian River. The two families would meet at some hammock, a clump of trees on higher ground. From there, the so-called hunters would go forth, mostly kids, and do a lot of shooting, not much killing. The birds would get tired of it, go into hiding, or go sit in the river where it was safe. In the meantime, the dads had killed enough for lunch and some extra to take home.

What's a coot, you may ask. If you have to ask, it shows you are a Yankee and nobody will claim kin to you in the south. A coot is a migratory water fowl that migrates to Florida around the month of November and leaves in March. They are a goofy looking bird with a black coat and white bill. While in the area, they feed on an aquatic grass called coot celery. Coots are good to eat if they come from this area, otherwise leave them alone.

The Briggs family came to Florida from Michigan. Cousin Evelyn Briggs Smith said the family lived in New England before going to Michigan. I don't recall anyone saying when the family moved to Florida, whether they came individually or as a group since each is an individual, with strong family ties. It could have gone either way.

Mr. Elmer Briggs and wife, Harriet, lived on the west bank of the Indian River south of Titusville, which (the home) is now across from Sears Town Mall. Their daughter Lila Briggs Rose and two children, Cleland and Janette Rose, lived with them until the beginning of World War II.

With the coming of the automobile after World War I, the people of North and South Merritt Islands knew they would need a bridge across the Banana Creek. They also knew they had to build it tall enough to accommodate the Widgeon, a large boat which carried supplies and people from Titusville to Canaveral Lighthouse and Chester Shoals Coast Guard Station. The bridge was known as the Humpback Bridge (see picture on *page 42).* *It was built on hard core, sabal palm piling. In 1936/37, the bridge was replaced, only to be replaced again by the shuttle crawlway. Dorr A. Briggs helped erect the first two bridges.*

The Canaveral Clubhouse and Coast Guard Station sites lie in the shadow of Launch Pad 39A.

North Merritt Island was never an island until the dredging of the Allenhurst Canal in the 1880's. This canal was dug and proved to be more practical as it was nearer to the deeper water of the Indian River.

There was very little or no factual knowledge about the Haulover Canal until the era of Dummitt and Turnbull, two early settlers. It is probable that Turnbull had a lot to do with digging of the first canal because he had workers when he

cut timber to ship to England. They said an underlying coquina shelf prevented them from going deeper in digging the Haulover Canal until they were able to acquire the mechanical means to do so. It is known that they had spans of oxen to haul the timber from the Indian River to the Mosquito Lagoon and rafted to the Ponce Inlet for shipment overseas.

There was a small oak hammock south of Dummitt Castle on the east side of Route 3 which was called Oxpen Hammock, a site used to pen the animals. This was claimed so by several of the old time settlers.

—H. Ray Benecke
Circa 1987

Orsino Baptist Church
Pictured above are members of the church, date unknown.

Original 18 charter members were: James H. Christy, James W. Christy, Edwina C. Christy, Dorr A. Briggs, Mrs. Dorr A. Briggs, Evart E. Briggs, Leslie K. Briggs, Floyd Briggs, Harvey Briggs, Evelyn Briggs, Mrs. Lillian M. Hutzlu, Miss Juanita Hutzlu, Miss Jettie Lollie, David H. Lollie, Arthur Lollie, Miss Eliza Quinton, and Charles Nauman.

1865 Mathushek studio grand piano purchased by my great-grandfather Henry Johan Benecke

History of the Mathushek Family Piano

The rosewood Mathushek studio grand piano was manufactured in New Haven, Connecticut. A family legend states that this piano, and a twin piano, were originally in a plantation in Atlanta, Georgia, and sold prior to the burning of Atlanta (1864) to a buyer in Jacksonville, Florida. I have researched this through the Piano Atlas and according to the serial number this piano was not manufactured until 1865.

When Lillie Benecke was eight years old, her father decided it was time for her to take piano lessons. He purchased the piano in Jacksonville, had it barged down the St. Johns River to the ocean, down the coast of Florida through the Haulover Canal to Merritt Island. When she was 16 years old, Lillie was told that she would have to earn money to buy her music. She earned the money by writing nature and hunting stories under the name of 'Uncle Dudley'. These stories were based on the experiences she had working as a hunting and fishing guide with her father on Merritt Island. They were published in Hunter, Trader, Trapper Magazine. She used the pen name 'Uncle Dudley' because she thought her stories would not be accepted if she submitted them under her own name.

When Lillie married and moved away, she had no way to transport the piano. The piano stayed at the old homestead until the family was forced to move when NASA began its expansion program. Lillie's brother Herman acquired the piano, dismantled it and stored it with other family possessions in his home.

In the early 1960's Lillie and her adult children rescued the piano, took it to Lakeland in the back of a pickup (it was in pieces) and had it restored. When Lillie and the piano were finally reunited in her home, she played it almost every day. She loved to play such hymns as *The Old Rugged Cross; We'll Meet in the Morning; In the Sweet By and By;* and T*he Little Brown Church.* Lillie also played many classical pieces her father had taught her. She purchased sheet music which is now in my possession.

Lillie continued to play the piano until her death in 1978. It remained silent until 2000 when Iris Caudill, Lillie's daughter, showed the piano to my sister Barbara Briggs Paugh and me. Later, I was able to purchase the piano from Iris and had it restored to its original condition. Much of the trim had to be reproduced; one of the scroll carvings was beyond repair and had to be duplicated. In the original restoration, some ivory keys had been replaced with plastic. These were then replaced by ivory, and the piano action was restored to original condition.

The piano now stately sits in my living room, overlooking the beautiful Great Smoky Mountains of North Carolina. I am taking piano lessons to learn to play this wonderful musical instrument. It is played occasionally by various profession-al musicians: two church organists, one of whom has per-formed on stage along with his opera singer wife; a 16 year old semi-professional young man from Sylva, North Carolina who plays 17 instru-ments; a young lady from Bulgaria who has a master's degree in musi-

cology and is a friend of our daughter-in-law, Teresa.

But the most famous performer associated with this piano was Liberace! While performing at The Lakeland Civic Center in Lakeland, Florida, he heard about the piano and petitioned the family to donate it to his piano museum. Iris Caudill refused his invitation. Thank you Iris for keeping this musical treasure in our family.

Iris Caudill

Zither made by Henry Johan Benecke
The zither is now in my possession.

68

This violin, a copy of an Antonio Stradivarius, belonged to a retired sea captain who had settled on the very northeast tip of North Merritt Island. As children, Lillie Benecke Caudill, her sisters and brother were greatly in awe of Captain John White. He was a weather-beaten man with white hair, a full white beard and a booming voice.

He lived in a large two-story house with a widow's walk on top where he would look out to sea with a spyglass to watch the various ships going by. He was skilled at playing the violin.

When Lillie expressed a desire to learn, Captain White told her that if she did, he would give her his old violin since his fingers were getting so stiff and bent with arthritis. Lillie learned to play the violin and Captain White kept his promise.

The violin is now in possession of Lillie's great-great grandson, Stuart Caudill V, who has lovingly restored it.

The Boys of North Merritt Island
Pictured left to right: Floyd Smith (married Evelyn Briggs), Leland Briggs,
Harvey Briggs, Evart Briggs, and Floyd Briggs

Mrs. Lolly in front of her house.
Mrs. Lolly was Floyd Briggs' mother-in-law.

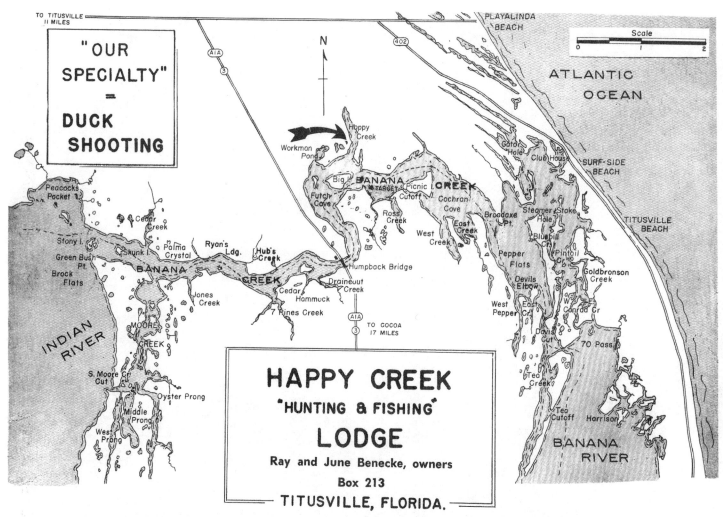

The map shows a coastal Florida region including the following labeled features:

TO TITUSVILLE 11 MILES

A1A · 3 · 402

PLAYALINDA BEACH

N

ATLANTIC OCEAN

Scale 0 1 2

"OUR SPECIALTY" = DUCK SHOOTING

Happy Creek · Workman Pond · Big I. · BANANA CREEK · TARGET · Picnic Cutoff · Futch Cove · Ross Creek · Cochran Cove · West Creek · East Creek · Broadaxe Pt. · Gator Hole · Club House · Steamer Stoke Hole · SURF-SIDE BEACH · TITUSVILLE BEACH · Bluebill Cr. · Pepper Flats · Pintail Cr. · Goldbronson Creek · Devils Elbow · West Pepper Cr. · East Pepper Cr. · W. Conrad Cr. · Davis Cut · Tea Creek · 70 Pass · Tea Cutoff · Harrison · BANANA RIVER

Peacocks Pocket · Cedar Creek · Stony I. · Green Bush Pt. · Skunk I. · Palma Crystal · Ryan's Ldg. · Hub's Creek · BANANA CREEK · Humpback Bridge · Draineout Creek · Cedar Hammock · Brock Flats · Jones Creek · 7 Pines Creek · INDIAN RIVER · MOORE CREEK · S. Moore Cr. Cut · Oyster Prong · Middle Prong · West Prong

A1A · 3 · TO COCOA 17 MILES

HAPPY CREEK
"HUNTING & FISHING"
LODGE
Ray and June Benecke, owners
Box 213
TITUSVILLE, FLORIDA.

MODERN HOUSEKEEPING COTTAGES · GUIDE SERVICE · BOATS · LAUNCHING

Arrow shows the location of the Happy Creek Hunting and Fishing Lodge. Ray and June Benecke continued to operate this business until 1962 when they were forced to sell the land to the government to become part of Kennedy Space Center. Ray and June sued the government and were both able to receive the cap amount placed on legal suits of this kind.

72

Ray and June Benecke, owners of Happy Creek Hunting and Fishing Lodge

The 'Betty Jo', built by Herman Benecke

The boat pictured here is a model of the 'Betty Jo' that Herman Benecke built for use to bring people to and from the mainland on Merritt Island.

Herman filled many requests from guests to build replicas of the Betty Jo.

74

A young June Benecke at left on the beach with friends

Catherine and Ray Benecke

Audrey, Catherine, Ray and June Benecke

Sitting on the motor launch at 'Uncle Herman's boat dock' in 1939.
This picture was taken on the east bank of Happy Creek, facing south.

Seated in front on floor of the boat is Daniel F. Deneff. From left: Ray Benecke with his arms on brother June's shoulders, Henry Benecke, Anna Laura Deneff, her mother Rose B. Deneff, Rose's husband John is standing behind her, Betty Benecke, Mary Crawford with her husband Herman seated behind her.

June Benecke Hurt In Hunting Accident

June Benecke, 12-year-old son of Herman Benecke of Merritt's Island near here, sustained a badly injured hand early Sunday morning when his shotgun was accidentally discharged.

The young boy was hunting with a party about eight or ten miles from home when the accident occurred at about seven o'clock. He was standing with his hand over the muzzle of his gun which was resting on the ground. The shot took away a portion of his hand, and it is believed that he may lose more of it. He was given first aid treatment here, and rushed to Florida Sanitarium at Winter Park for surgical attention. He was taken to that city by Reginald Wager.

June Benecke had just been injured in a hunting accident when the picture on the previous page was taken. This is a copy of the newspaper article.

—Courtesy of Titusville Star-Advocate

79

Ways and By-ways of North Merritt Island
by Ray Benecke
1993

The early settlers on the south part of North Merritt Island depended completely on Banana Creek for their livelihood. It was a means of transportation by boat to and from Titusville. It also connected the Indian River to the headwaters of Banana River. Some of the early settlers who lived on the east bank of Banana River arrived around the Civil War era. Their main source of income was orange groves. Other settlers planted pineapples which did very well at first. Later the pineapples froze during the big 1894 freeze. Some of the more notable families were: Quarterman, Skyler, Peterson, Penney, White, and Burns. This area was known as Cape Canaveral, or the Canaveral peninsula. Much later it became known as the Eastern Range.

Banana Creek was the dividing line between North and South Merritt Island. It also served as a dividing line between Commission Districts 2 and 5, where it remained for many years.

There was an abundance of game, fish and fowl which helped the people eke out a living. Others trapped animals and alligators for hides. Cattle were introduced too. Some tried and succeeded by planting orange groves, but this proved to be hard work clearing the land as it had to be cleared with hand tools.

June Benecke shoveling mullet

Although there was an abundance of fish, commercial fishing on Banana Creek did not prove practical on a large scale until the arrival of power boats. There was some fishing done in the colder winter months. But for the rest of the year, the distance to the fish house was too far.

June Benecke

With the coming of the power boat, large barges were built and loaded with ice. These boats were anchored one and one-half miles south of Happy Creek at a place called the Divide. These run boats were operated by Henry Benecke and Cyrus Ryan (Ryan's Landing). After catches were made, the run boats were towed to the markets in Titusville for a fee.

In the year of 1912, the government opened several thousand acres on South Merritt Island to homesteaders. This land had been established as a game reserve by President Teddy Roosevelt but was later opened for homesteading by President Robert Taft.

Just north of NASA's Vehicle Assembly Building is an area on Banana Creek which was known as Briggs Landing. The settlers brought their supplies by boat from Titusville to this landing, where they were unloaded and hauled by wagon to homesteads in the interior of the island. One of these settlers, Mr. Elliot who was also one of the haulers, told of a panther that trailed along with him and his team of oxen like a dog several times a week. He never worried as he considered it harmless, "just curious."

About two miles north of this site was a settlement known as Sacketts. Mr. Sackett was one of the first settlers in the area. My grandfather Henry Benecke was acquainted with him. After Mr. Sackett died, this area was settled by the Oscar Warley, Henry Futch, and Fred Nauman families. The area is now used by NASA for invited guests to view the shuttle launches.

Approximately two miles northeast of the above area is Happy Creek where my grandfather homesteaded. A number of years (1870's) before my grandfather arrived, a Mr. Wager homesteaded, cleared land, and planted sugar cane on adjacent property. When the cane was harvested, the juice was squeezed into a large cast iron vat and boiled into syrup, molasses and sugar.

A folk story tells that one of the workers had a birthday and the others decided to give him a party. The squeezing from the cane provided plenty of alcohol (rum). After the "happy party", they decided to call the area Happy Creek and Happy Hammock. On one occasion, they had to make a trip to the mainland for a load of pitch pine for their syrup boilings. When they returned they began unloading. Mr. Wager decided to go ahead and fix supper. When the others arrived at camp, Mr. Wager had disappeared. His disappearance is still a mystery with lots of theories.

At the mouth of Happy Creek was a tract of land acquired from the Pliney Sheffield estate (1906) by Calvin Flood and family. This area was later bought by the S.E. Bailey family who resided there for many years. In 1944, my brother, C.J. (June) Benecke and I bought it and built Happy Creek Hunting and Fishing Lodge (see map on page 72).

Several miles east of Happy Creek, on the coast during the late 1800's, the government built the Chester Shoals Coast Guard Station because of the treacherous shoals that had wrecked many early sailing vessels. Orlando Quarterman was the first caretaker. Upon his retirement, his son, George Quarterman was placed in charge until World War II. It had been used as a coast guard training station during World War I. It was used to billet patrols to help prevent German saboteurs from infiltrating through the area.

82

Nearby, the Canaveral Hunting Club was built during the 1880's. It was formed by several millionaires from Boston, Massachusetts. They resided there during the winter months and left it with caretakers for the rest of the year. My father and grandfather worked for them at various times. (Henry Johan worked as a carpenter and a gunsmith). Launch Pad 39A now stands at this site.

Except for the Banana Creek and Haulover Canal areas, most of the inland area of the north island started development around 1912 as South Merritt Island did. The greatest influx of people came shortly after World War I ended.

The history of the Haulover Canal area goes back to the time the Spanish lived in Florida. It was said to have been used by raiders to escape pursuing naval forces. Small boats were hauled across this narrow strip of land that lies between the Mosquito Lagoon and the Indian River. Attempts were made by the earlier settlers to dig a small canal by hand but they were only partly successful because of the coquina rock shelf. After this small canal was dug, they could bring larger boats across with the aid of oxen. Later a dredge was brought in to dig a navigable channel at the present site which is approximately one mile west of the old canal. The new canal was built by private investors and a toll was collected.

Later it was bought by the government as

part of the inland navigational system.

Max Hoeck was one of the workers during this time. He resided at the Dummitt Castle. On his days off, he would scout for a home site. He found a place to homestead on the south bank of the Mosquito Lagoon. This site is near Edies Cove or nearly two miles north of Playalinda Beach. Mr. Hoeck did well after moving to his homestead. He hired young men from Germany by paying for their passage to America and letting them repay him by clearing his property. He planted orange groves and kept bees.

June Benecke, Henry J. Benecke and Richard Hochreither

It is told that he sold wine in Titusville off his boat from large wooden barrels to anyone with a gallon jug. At that time this was legal. Mr. Hoeck helped my grandfather Henry Benecke find his place on Happy Creek.

As the new settlers came, so did the desire for automobiles. The people started clearing right-of-way for roads to widen existing trails. When possible they followed section or township lines. All the men who were able to formed neighbor-hood work groups and built their roads by donating one day a week, mostly weekends. Sometimes the ladies prepared a picnic lunch near the work site. Later, the county built the beach road, also known as Route 402. With the construction of the John Walker Toll Bridge, it was easier for people to have access to Titusville and for people from Titusville to go to the beaches.

The road running south from the beach road was Happy Creek Road or Range 37 Road. It served the people of the Happy Creek area. West of the present (1993) Route 3 was as dirt road that ran south approximately three miles, then ran east two miles, then again turned south crossing Banana Creek and continued to Orsino. This road was later straightened to become State Road 3 and is crossed by the shuttle landing strip. Further west was a road that was later called Wisconsin Village Road. It was built by Chester Schnopp and neigh-bors. In this area, going north from 402 was a road called the Bulb Farm Road. This road ran north to

Allenhurst or Haulover Canal. Most of the road was later taken over by Route 3. The area around these junctions was known as Wilson. The Wilson School was the meeting place for residents living on the island. They voted, had dances, suppers, and met to discuss civic issues. This was during the 1920's, 1930's and 1940's. In the early 1950's, the North Merritt Island Community Building was erected.

Living on North or South Merritt Island wasn't what most people would call easy. Mosquitoes at times made life miserable. The land was hard to clear by the first settlers. To clear an acre of ground would take one man thirty days as it had to be done with hand tools. Roads were two-track sand traps during dry spells. They became mug bogs when wet. Most of the people accepted the good with the bad, and held the optimistic view that everything would get better, and it usually did.

Some of the people who settled on the island couldn't find jobs and had to move on. Others held onto their property but moved to be near their workplace or business. There were those who could stay because of their occupations. They would survive; and because that was all they ever wanted, they stayed.

Herman Benecke cleaning ducks

The ducks were cleaned and canned, and the feathers were used for bedding and pillows

84

Our First Traffic Jam?

"**W**ell," I said, flopping down next to the Old Timer in the cool shade of his porch, "The darned..."

Interrupting me with a raised hand and big grin he replied, "I know, I know, it's the traffic that's made you late again.

"On May Day, 1917, the first bridge across the Indian River from Cocoa to Merritt Island was opened officially, and here's a picture of the crowd of people and autos that came to celebrate the occasion. The bridge extended from the foot of Harrison Street, across the river to Merritt where modern day State Road 520 lands today, and while it was welcome for its aid to the citrus industry, which could now truck

CHUCK REED

THOSE DAYS REMEMBERED

picked fruit over to packing houses in Cocoa for loading directly onto northbound trains, it was several more years before the Beach Road crossed Merritt Island and the Banana River and the development of Cocoa Beach could begin."

With a chuckle, the Old Timer said, "I reckon it was many years before that much traffic tried to cross the river at the same time, and no one seemed to be in a hurry or cared whether they get across or not!"

THE FIRST BRIDGE TO CROSS THE INDIAN RIVER to connect Cocoa and Merritt Island extended from the end of Harrison Street to where State Road 520 enters Merritt Island

Article showing the first bridge built that crossed the Indian River from Cocoa to Merritt Island, May 1, 1917

—Article courtesy Florida Today Newspaper, May 31, 2001

Lena Benecke Briggs is admiring her nine grandchildren outside of her home on Merritt Island.

I am seated on the step, third from right. My sister Barbara is fifth from right,
and my two older sisters, Celia and Shirley (holding her dress), are standing next to Lena.

Evart Elmer Briggs and his baby brother Harvey, circa 1924

Harvey Briggs

SCHOOL DAYS 1950-51
TITUSVILLE

Leland L. Briggs – High School Photo

"Desoto Beach was somewhere between Launch Pad A and Launch Pad B. Club House Creek Road is where the Cape Canaveral Clubhouse was located. That is where I had my first swim in a swimming pool. It was artesian well water. I almost drowned once in that pool – I remember going under water. I can't remember who pulled me out, only that it was a close call!"

—Leland Briggs

Leland Briggs at Ft. Campbell Kentucky, 1954

Harvey, Lena, Dorr, Leland, Evelyn and Evart Briggs

Harvey had been a passenger in a vehicle driven by his brother Leslie that crashed head-on with another vehicle on Cocoa Beach in 1939. Leslie was killed and Harvey suffered a severe head injury that left him in a coma for a month and resulted in some loss of brain function.

Leland was four years old when his brother Leslie died. He remembers that evening as being very traumatic. His mother Lena woke him up and dressed him in a gray jumpsuit. "I'll never forget that. It is in my memory and will never go away. I can still remember looking at my brother's face in the coffin."

TITUSVILLE STAR-ADVOCATE

LETE LOCAL NEWS   TITUSVILLE, FLORIDA, FRIDAY, JUNE 23, 1939   PUBLISHED TUESDAYS AND FRIDAYS

ONE DEAD IN COCOA BEACH AUTO CRASH

Nine Others Are Injured In Beach Accident Thursday Night

FOUR BADLY HURT

Three Brothers Figure In The Mishap

One person is dead and nine others are injured—four of them in a Melbourne hospital—following a sideswipe automobile crash about ten o'clock last night on Cocoa Beach.

Sheriff H. T. Williams, one of the officers investigating the crash, listed Leslie Briggs, 21-year-old son of Mr. and Mrs. Dorr A. Briggs, of Orsino district, Merritt Island, as the dead and two of his brothers in a serious condition.

Others involved in the crash and listed by Sheriff Williams are Harvey and Floyd Briggs, Oscar and Curtis Futch and Roy Leonard all of Merritt Island. And occupants of a second car, Ina Miller, Grace Shokkey, Sid Henderson and Chartres Cowart all of Cocoa.

Four In Hospital

Attaches at the Brevard County hospital in Melbourne said today that the condition of four of the occupants of the two cars, were unchanged, and listed those who were rushed there last night as, Ina Miller, Curtis and Oscar Futch, and Harvey Briggs, all seriously injured. The other passengers of the cars who were injured were released by Cocoa physicians after first-aid treatment.

According to information available here this morning, the two automobiles were traveling in opposite directions on the beach, about two and one half miles north of the beach Casino, when one of the cars swerved to the left, apparently in an effort to avoid striking the other, and the oncoming vehicle did practically the same.

Sheriff Williams said the two cars seemed to have collided in the midst of a left and right swing.

When the accident was investigated this morning, the tides had swelled out almost covering both cars with water and it was difficult to determine much about how the accident really occured.

Williams said he hardly thought an inquest necessary, but that he was awaiting the outcome of the condition of the occupants in the Melbourne hospital before deciding upon this part of the accident.

Road Patrolman E. K. Griggs, also aided in the investigation, along with Williams and members of the Cocoa police force.

—Courtesy of Titusville Star Advocate
Friday, June 23, 1939

CRASH VICTIM IS BURIED SUNDAY

Others Reported To Be Slightly Improved

Unconscious Still

Miss Irma Brubaker, nurse at the Brevard County Hospital in Melbourne, said late last night that Harvey Briggs, 15, one of the nine injured in a Cocoa Beach automobile crash last Thursday night that claimed the life of one is still unconscious. One of the other three who was seriously injured—Ine Miller, 18—is also still unconscious, the nurse said.

Leslie Biggs, 21-year-old son of Mr. and Mrs. Dorr A. Briggs, Orsino, North Merritt Island, was buried Sunday afternoon in Memorial Park cemetary.

Last rites were earlier conducted at the Koon Funeral Home here, with the Rev. C. K. Byerly, pastor of the Orsino Baptist church officiating.

Young Briggs died instantly last Thursday night on Cocoa Beach, several miles north of Ocean Lodge, after the car in which he and several companions rode collided with another automobile when each of them swerved away from the coast side apparently to avoid striking the other.

Nine others were injured in the crash which claimed the life of young Briggs, formerly a Titusville High School student.

Four of the occupants — one a brother of the dead man, Harvey Briggs, 15, — is still in the Brevard hospital at Melbourne. Ina Miller, 18, also of Merritt Island, Oscar and Curtis Futch were the other three who sustained injuries necessary to send them to the hospital. They were reported improved Saturday, but still not out of danger, attaches at the institution said.

Sheriff H. T. Williams said today, after talking with the parents of the Briggs boys, that an inquest is termed "unnecessary".

Surviving Briggs are his parents, Mr. and Mrs. Dorr A. Briggs, four brothers and a sister, Harvey, Floyd, Leeland, and Everitt and Miss Evelyn Briggs, all of Orsino.

—Courtesy of Titusville
Star Advocate

Evart Briggs with his mother Lena, and a family friend, George Honaker

Stuart, Lillie and Alice Caudill at Happy Creek

Stuart H. Caudill, Sr., Willie, Lillie, Iris (in front), and Hagard (Stuart H., Jr.) Caudill

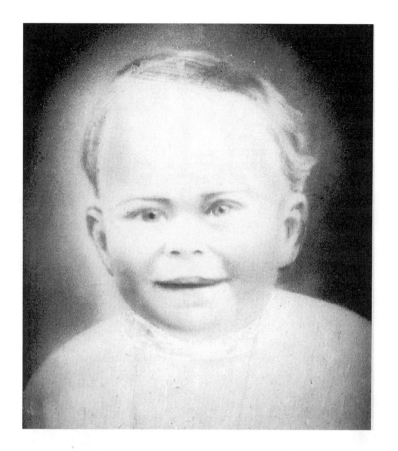

*Juanette Caudill, the fourth child of
Lillie Caudill. Juanette died of colitis
when she was nine months old.*

*Stuart Hagard Caudill, Alice Caudill
and William Caudill
on February 4, 1921.*

Alice and Juanette were stricken with colitis and died within three days of each other. Alice died at age nine on February 3, 1924. Juanette died at age nine months on February 6, 1924.

William was married to Ruth Hagan for 50 years and died at age 78 in 1994 in Lakeland, Florida. Stuart Hagard passed away at the age of 85 in November, 2003.

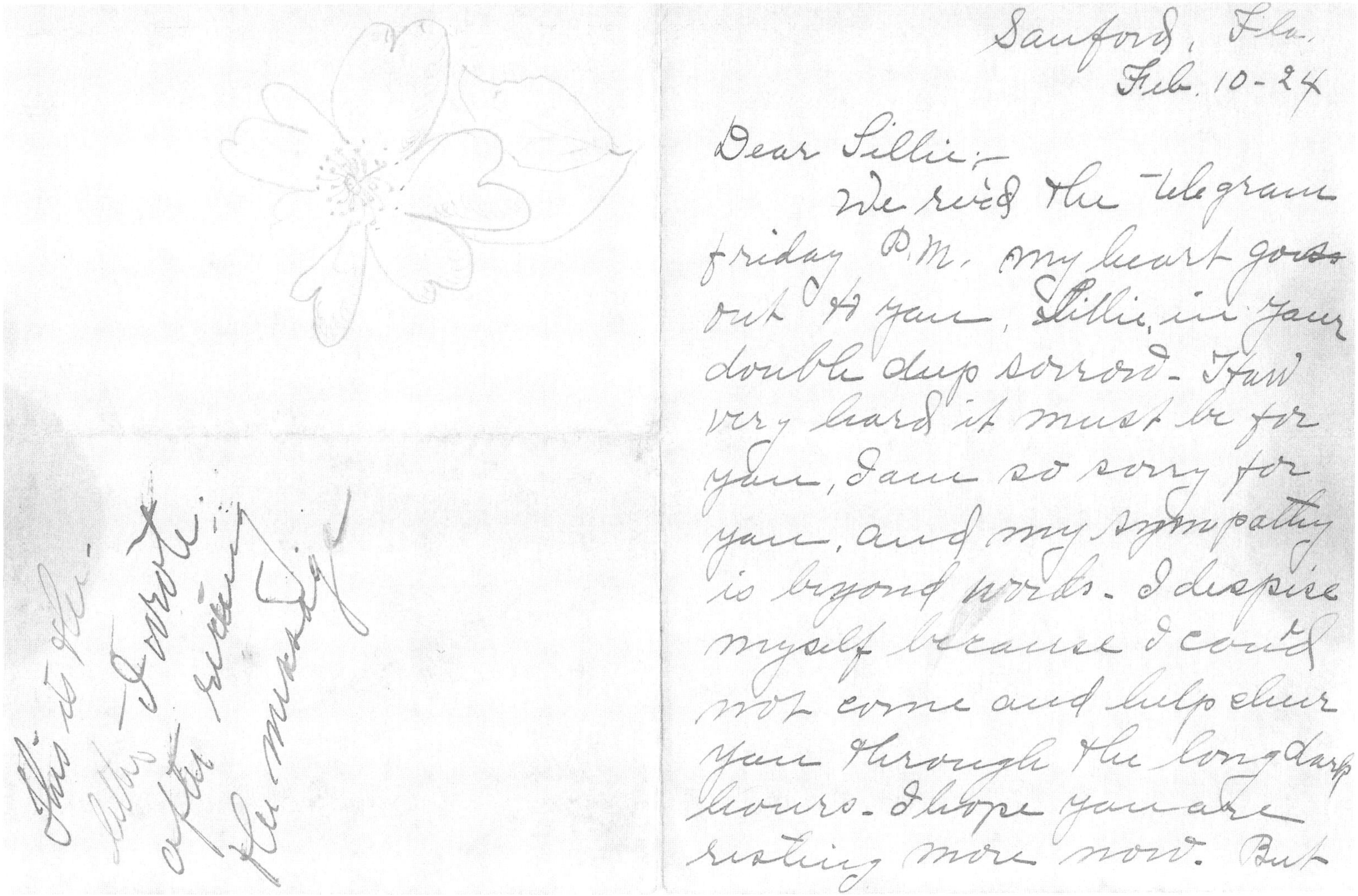

Sanford, Fla.
Feb. 10-24

Dear Lillie:-
We rec'd the telegram friday P.M. my heart goes out to you, Lillie, in your double deep sorrow. How very hard it must be for you, I am so sorry for you, and my sympathy is beyond words. I despise myself because I could not come and help cheer you through the long dark hours. I hope you are resting more now. But

This is the letter I wrote after receiving the message

After the death of her young children Juanette and Alice,
Lillie received this heart-felt letter from her sister Laura.
—Side 1 of 2—

perhaps you are not too not

I don't see how I could
ever enjoy any thing again
if I lost one of mine. I
would have come but I knew
I would be too late for the
funeral and besides it was
awful cold to take the baby
having a cold. I hope
Anna was with you.

Tillie tell me what caused
her death. When the messenger
boy handed me the teligram
I was so shocked and
nervous I could not talk
and was nervous for hours

after. How you must
suffer through your
great loss.

I see mike coming
and I will close so I can
send this to morrow.

Write me, dear sister,
for I am so sorry for
you. A kiss for dear little
dead Juanette and you I
am ever your sister

Laura

I would have written
Saturday but had no envelope in
the house.

"She got her man!"
Floyd Lane Smith (Evelyn Briggs' husband) and Iris Caudill (6'3")

Taken in the early 1950's on Merritt Island, Floyd jokingly told Iris to arrest him for this picture.
Being the first woman Deputy Constable in the state of Florida, Iris worked for Pat Gordon when he was
both the Constable and Sheriff for Polk County, Florida.

ABWA Units Honor Top Women

ABWA'S WOMAN OF THE YEAR
. . . is Miss Iris Caudill

New Woman of the Year for Lakeland Imperial Chapter, American Business Women's Association is Miss Iris Caudill.

The announcement of her selection came at a recent meeting. She was chosen from nominations submitted to Mrs. O. B. Hannah, last year's winner, on the basis of her service to ABWA and her civic and church activities.

Miss Caudill is a native of Polk County and received her education in Lakeland schools. She recently completed a course in machine stenography at Polk Junior College.

She has served Lakeland Imperial Chapter as president, corresponding secretary, program chairman, bulleting chairman, photographer and district meeting delegate.

Miss Caudill is also a member of Lakeland's Coordinating Council of Women's Organizations, Lakeland Legal Secretaries and Southside Baptist Church. She is employed as secretary and bookkeeper in the office of Constable Pat Gordon and was Florida's first woman deputy constable.

Meanwhile, ABWA's Heart O' Florida Chapter in Winter Haven has picked its own Woman of the Year.

She is Mrs. T. C. Benson, assistant manager of Winter Haven office of the Florida State Employment Service.

Mrs. Benson is a charter member of ABWA and also belongs to Green Thumb Garden Club, Ridge Orchid Society, Business and Professional Women's Club, International Association of Personnel in Employment Security, Florida State Employees Association and Inman Park Baptist Church.

She was presented a trophy by Miss Martha Ethridge, the chapter's retiring president. Mrs. Jo Baugh was chairman of the committee to name the new Woman of the Year.

—Courtsey of The Lakeland Ledger

Iris was the fifth of six children of Lillie and Stuart Caudill, Sr. She lived with her single-parent mother and from the age of ten, helped with the chores and took care of her younger brother David.

Here And There About Lakeland

BEAUTY AND THE LAW—
Criminals will find it almost a pleasure to be "pinched" by this newest "arm of the law" in Lakeland. She is Miss Iris Caudill, who has been authorized to serve as deputy to Constable Pat Gordon. Although she has full power of arrest, Miss Caudill is expected to confine her duties to serving legal papers handled through Gordon's office.

Iris' achievements include being selected Woman of the Year for the Legal Secretaries in 1972, and had the distinction of being elected Woman of the Year of the American Business Woman's Association, Lakeland Imperial Chapter, in 1963.

—Courtsey of The Lakeland Ledge

David Caudill

These pictures were taken at the home of Johnny Stalder on Merritt Island. The gun pictured was made by Henry Johan Benecke, and was a revolver-rifle.

Johnny Stalder

VOLUME XIX   DECEMBER, 1909   No. 3

HUNTER TRADER TRAPPER

Charles C. Kinch and Black Bear which he killed in
White Mountains of New Hampshire.

$1.00 A YEAR   AN ILLUSTRATED MAGAZINE OF INFORMATION   10c A COPY
COLUMBUS, OHIO.

*"Uncle Dudley" submitted articles to Hunter,
Trader, Trapper, a magazine first published in
Columbus, Ohio in 1900.*

HUNTING IN FLORIDA

By UNCLE DUDLEY

ONCE I had an acquaintance named Tom O'Bears. He was pretty slow and easy going and could go to sleep at his work. One winter O'Bears invited me to accompany him on a hunting expedition to the State of Florida. I of course readily accepted the invitation. O'Bears went first, as I had some business which detained me, but I decided to follow in a week or so. I managed to get away at the end of a week with another friend who insisted on going with me. I could not refuse his request so allowed him to go along.

We arrived in Titusville, Fla., and were met at the station by one of O'Bears' most intimate friends, Mr. Phil Garlick. He was a tall, lank fellow—a regular "Florida Cracker," and he took us to O'Bears' camp which was some six or seven miles from town. When we were in speaking distance of the shore we heard O'Bears' yell, "Come in fellers and have some 'gator steak." Well, we landed, baggage and all, and after being cordially received I entered Mr. O'Bears' camp. And now I am going to give a description of it: There was a clearing about forty feet square and in the center was a shanty made of oak boughs and palmetto leaves. The shanty was very attractive. It had only one opening which was door, window and chimney. There were a couple of beds on the ground, two or three trunks and a small fireplace. On the outside was a camp stove, a table and a few old boxes which served as chairs. A few pots and frying pans and a cat made up the household of this grand camp. O'Bears, after showing us the wonders of his camp, began bragging about "that cross-eyed cat" of his. "For," says he, "I am certainly blessed with that cat as it keeps the rats and mice away from here and it won't steal a thing."

It being rather late in the afternoon and being pretty tired from our journey, we decided not to go out for a hunt that day. We chewed the rag until O'Bears thought it was about time for supper, so he and Mr. Garlick went to work and made a fire, peeled some potatoes and sliced some fresh pork. This done O'Bears said we had to go and get some water from the well which was about a hundred and fifty yards from camp. He said it was best to have plenty of water in camp over night for there was no telling but that some one would want a drink during the night. So all four of us followed O'Bears to the well which in fact was nothing but an old 'gator's hole from which the owners had long since departed. We got some of the water and it looked like black coffee, but the taste was all right, although it contained a little sulphur. Well, soon we were back in camp but upon entering we all received a shock, for there was "Cross-eyes" on the table, having a great time with the sliced bacon. "Great Spoons," cried O'Bears, "who would have thought it," and seizing the cat by the tail he sent her into a clump of Spanish bayonets. Some time after when he wanted the cat back, he set a steel trap for her and she got caught by her head, thus ending her days. After O'Bears had cooled down, he and Mr. Garlick made a fine supper. O'Bears always was a splendid cook. I enjoyed my first supper in Florida very much.

Mr. Pill Garlick owned a farm about two miles from camp and as soon as we had finished supper he took his leave and went home. We all soon retired and slept like 'possums all night.

Early next day after breakfast O'Bears said that we would go to Pill Garlick's and invite him to go with us for a hunt. We took our guns and went down to the landing where we found O'Bears' boat in good condition, and after half an hour's good rowing we arrived at Pill's wharf. We had

just put our feet on the wharf when I received a shock which nearly threw me in the water. The cause of this was that I saw two dogs, that were indeed a fearful sight—so thin that they looked like skeletons and could hardly be seen end on. They came towards us and had to lean up against each other while they barked at us, in order to keep from falling into the water.

Mr. Garlick said he was ready to go for a hunt. He had some traps set and, therefore, he would go with us. He got his gun and ammunition and soon we were off on an all day's hunt. But first Mr. Garlick wished to go to his traps, so of course we all accompanied him and we learned a good many new things about trapping. We went to a dozen traps but there was nothing in them and we were on the point of going away when Mr. Garlick remembered that there was another trap a few hundred yards away from the rest. We went there and found that an old otter had been pretty careless where he had put his foot and therefore got caught in the trap. We all wanted to shoot the otter but Mr. Garlick objected. He had a short, heavy stick with which he killed all the animals caught in his traps and so he wanted to kill an otter with it also. He went around the otter several times attempting to hit him on the head but the creature was too sly for Pill. At last when Pill was off his guard the otter leaped at him and set his teeth into Pill's shins causing him to give a yell of pain. "Great spoons," he yelled, "Let go, you black one, if you kill me I'll knock you in the head." O'Bears used his gun and he attempted to strike the otter but quite accidentally hit Pill's other foot. "Now," he screamed, "He's got my other foot, too" and then he began using anything but Sunday school talk. Billy Goote, who was one of our party, finally managed to kill the otter thus freeing poor Pill. O'Bears and I pulled him out of the mud and he began to look for the marks left by the otter's teeth on his shins but he could not find any. This surprised us all, but we soon saw what had hurt Mr. Garlick—the otter had torn his shoes quite badly and this meant a new pair of shoes for Mr. Garlick. Well, anyway Pill took the hide off the otter and we hunted for more game, but did not get any. Pretty soon we went back to camp, leaving Pill at his place.

We had dinner and then decided to go for a coon hunt out in the marshes. We started off with one gun and a lantern, for as it was already late we decided to stay out until after sundown. Passing Mr. Garlick's place we borrowed his coon dog. He said the dog was rather thin but he guessed he could stand a little tramp out in the woods. So we went to the marshes and hunted for coon. We found plenty of signs but we did not get even a peep at a coon. We soon knew the reason for this—Pill Garlick's dog was a regular "yaller" dog, good for nothing. How we found out was in this way: A rat of pretty good size ran out of the grass just in front of the dog. Well, I will never forget how that dog ran. He just gave a howl and lit out for home with his tail between his legs,

C. S. Inman with Deer Killed on a Four Days' Hunt in Williams Co., North Dakota.

"Uncle Dudley" was Lillie Benecke Caudill.

but Pill Garlick told us later that the dog never came home, so I guess he is running yet, if he is not starved to death.

We killed a few jack rabbits and also a number of small snipes and with these we had to be content and returned to camp as it was growing dark and without a dog it was useless to hunt for coon.

Soon we were on our way back talking while we walked along and O'Bears often used strong words to Pill's "yaller" dog.

While we were walking on a path I saw something that looked like a paper bag and not being able to see it quite plainly in the dusk, I gave it a kick with my foot to get it from the road. It was a little heavier and softer than paper and soon we became conscious of a very strong smell which was worse than limburger cheese and made us light out for camp. We changed our clothes in a hurry and hung the hunting suits on a tree near the stove. Well, we washed the mud from our boots and cleaned our gun and then O'Bears started to get supper. We had a pretty hot fire going and soon we began smelling the skunk again. I knew it was the clothes back of the stove, but O'Bears and Billy said in serious tones, "Say, pard, that skunk must surely have followed us to camp. I can smell it again."

Well, this ended one day's hunt and a grand time we all had of it.

102

FLORIDA SKUNK INCIDENT.

There are quite an abundance of skunk here in Florida. Trappers are very glad of this but I doubt if the poultry man is, for skunk are as fond of chickens as their next door neighbor, the raccoon and opossum.

Well there was a skunk visiting around our poultry yard for some time partaking very freely of the fatest hens, but we could never get a peep at him as we did not know where he stayed. One day I had some ducks to pick. I went out to the wood shed and began picking the feathers into an old flour barrel. It was nearly full of feathers so I put my hand in to press them down. Suddenly I felt something move in the barrel. Thinking it was a rat or mouse I dropped the duck which I had in my hand and got hold of the broom that stood near. Nothing came out of the barrel so I took it and carried it in the open and called for a gun. A half a dozen came running with a gun each and asked what was up. I told them there was a rat in the barrel and they could try and kill it.

I took the barrel and turned it up side down then rolled it over. There was a cloud of feathers and something ran out toward the scrumb but it was a skunk and no rat. They shot six times at him but no one hit him. They only filled the air with bullets and every one wondered why, for the bullets were thick enough. After a while I carried the barrel back to the wood shed and put some more feathers in it. Next morning I went back to see if the skunk was there. I put my hand in the barrel but not very far when suddenly the air was filled with a disagreeable smell and I was quite sure that the skunk was there.

I took the barrel carefully up and carried it back to where we had it before. Then I went and asked my mother if she wanted to have some fun. She said "yes, sure.' I told her to get her gun and come and kill that skunk. "Where is my cannon," she asked. I did not want to get skunked with the old thing so I turned the barrel over and rolled it a bit then I got behind mother for protection. The skunk came out, but when she was about 3 feet from the barrel she stopped. Mother took careful aim and fired. Something funny happened then. The force of the shot was so great that it carried the skunk back into the barrel and out through the other end, taking the bottom and all the feathers along.

I think mother must have pulled the trigger of old "trusty" awful hard to cause so great a power. Mother is an expert at shooting, and when it comes to hunting no one can get ahead of her. She killed a dozen quail with one shot and one time she killed a big black bear.

Mother and I used to have lots of fun hunting together. She would kill the ducks and coots and I waded into the ponds and got them out. This was when I was little and could not shoot a gun. Now I am big and can hunt and shoot all I want and have lots of fun too. I have three firearms, a double barrel shot gun, 12 gauge, a 32 caliber rifle and a 32 caliber Smith & Wesson revolver. I find these guns pretty handy.

L. E. B., Brevard Co., Fla.

In each article, "Uncle Dudley" expertly described the hunting and fishing excursions of guests who visited Merritt Island. The guide service was owned and operated by my great-grandfather, Henry J. Benecke. "Uncle Dudley" was his daughter Lillie, who at the age of 16 in 1909, had to earn money to pay for her piano lessons and sheet music. Iris Caudill, Lillie's daughter furnished the first article for the book from among Lillie's belongings. The second one I acquired through on-line auctions of Hunter, Trader, Trapper Magazines.

The Saturn V being moved from the VAB building (in background) to Launch Pad 39A Kennedy Space Center. It is fully assembled on the Mobile Launcher on the crawler.
The second Apollo Saturn V rocket is being assembled in the VAB bay on the right side of the building.
Between the two is the third Mobile Launcher.

—Courtesy of Space Coast News, Kennedy Space Center

The Briggs homestead was located near both of these sites.

*—Courtesy of Space Coast News,
Kennedy Space Center*

*"The Roy Roberts family home passes
in defeat before the gigantic Vertical
(Vehicle) Assembly Building."*

Roy Roberts's two-story frame and coquina rock home was moved to Scottsmoor in 1971. Mr. Roberts still travels to the island five or six days a week to take care of his groves. In his land settlement with the government, Mr. Roberts retained the right to own and maintain his groves in restricted areas.

"I love the island. I go down to Happy Creek every once in a while. I just have to go visit those other places every once in a while, too. Like I say, I love the island; it's kind of like a memory walk."

Roy Roberts, Jr.—October 2003

Roy Roberts home in Scottsmore, 2004

The man in this article is Roy Roberts, Sr., a friend and neighbor of the Briggs and Benecke families on Merritt Island. Roy Roberts, Jr. still maintains the family orange groves on Merritt Island with the help of his son. Roy Roberts, Jr. lives in the family home that was moved from Merritt Island to Scottsmoor.

Prohibition

■ **On the books:** Brevard County was never completely dry during the Prohibition days of 1920 to 1933.

■ **On the beach:** Rum runners especially liked to sneak into Sebastian Inlet to unload their shipments. Boats came from the west end of Grand Bahama and slipped quietly onto the beach, where burlap bags were unloaded into a Buick Master Six Roadmaster with the rear seat removed. Other times the boats would hide by the Mullet Creek islands during the day before heading north.

When it was rumored a boat was coming in, some Melbourne men would go to watch, and even purchase a case of good Scotch or Canadian whisky.

■ **On the road:** The rum runners drove their cars north to present day Melbourne, along a road that was nothing more than sand with holes filled in with shells. From there they headed out to the big cities — Memphis, Cincinnati, Chicago, Kansas City and St. Louis.

■ **By train:** Another source of booze was the Havana Special train, which stopped at every town in the county. Luggage trunks of those heading north marked "Wearing Apparel" gurgled suspiciously when being unloaded from the Havana Special. Baggage han-

For FLORIDA TODAY

Former Titusville Sheriff Roy Roberts displays the remnants of a bootleg liquor still he confiscated. He is holding the kettle, or cooker, and the coil is on the ground by the rear bumper.

dlers quickly learned a lot of baggage doubled in weight when people came back from Cuba.

■ **Local efforts:** When Prohibition became law, many local citizens went into the "bootlegging" trade. They made "moonshine," and the location of the stills were well known.

In the 1920s, Roy Couch founded the Couch Manufacturing Co. on the shores of the Indian River in Grant. During Prohibition, his plant also serv-

iced the engines of the rum runners' boats. It is not certain whether this was done "under cover" or openly, but all the employees were aware of it. Couch, it is said, received choice liquor from the Bahamas in exchange for this service.

Sources: "Pioneer Settlers of Melbourne" by Fred Hopwood and "Images of America: North Brevard County" by John Manning and Robert Hudson.

—Article submitted by Ray Benecke

107

This saddle was used by Mrs. Roy Roberts, Sr. in 1924 – 1925 as she delivered the mail on Merritt Island. Her uncle returned with it after World War 1.

Her son, Roy Roberts, Jr. used the same saddle as a youngster tending to his father's groves on Merritt Island. The Roberts' place was located one mile south of Orsino, approximately six miles south of the Briggs' property. Roy used to ride the same school bus as the Briggs children, but had to walk home or hitch a ride as "the bus went only as far south as the Briggs' place."

Canaveral Boom Is Bust for Some

By DAN BROWN
Cocoa Bureau Chief

TITUSVILLE BEACH — Happy Creek is a sad place now.

Expanding Cape Canaveral is going to gobble it up —uproot the pioneer family that discovered it nearly a century ago.

"And," said Mrs. June Benecke, "we're sick about it. We haven't eaten a decent meal since this thing was announced.

"Beneckes have been living here more than 80 years. They built everything here. We don't have any place to go."

The Beneckes aren't alone.

About 300 families are in the way of Cape Canaveral

which is to grow nearly five times and become a moon rocket base — a center for a great Florida boom.

And they're asking: "How can we afford it?"

J. H. Benecke, patriarch of the Happy Creek clan, doesn't know.

"We're already looking for land," he said. "But the only thing we can find that we like — land not one bit better than this — costs $2,000 an acre, and we can't afford it. We'll be lucky if we get $300 an acre for what we've got."

* * *

THE BENECKE land is orange groves and the base for a family commercial fishing business and fishing-hunting guides. It is land built up out of the great marshes of North Merritt Island.

Pioneer Patriarch H. J. Benecke
...family displaced after 75 years

—Herald Staff Photos by DAN BROWN

Moving Merchant Harold Merrifield
...no sale, but going out of business

"And how," asked Mrs. Benecke (the old man's daughter-in-law), "Do you compensate a man for land he built himself? Or make up for a business so old that they used to fish under sail here?"

The Beneckes and a few of their neighbors are real pioneers — people who got their land by improving it under the Homestead Act that settled much of the American West.

But even the newpioneers here share a problem with the Beneckes — land prices are booming nearby to costs far above what people expect to get for the land they're going to lose.

Mrs. Jean Carroll, a three-year Titusville Beach resident, had been thinking of buying a $900 Titusville lot before the Cape expansion was announced.

After the announcement, the price jumped to $2,000.

Harold Merrifield — proprietor of a thriving Titusville Beach combination general store, restaurant, package store, gasoline station and three business buildings — thinks his business will die no matter what he gets for the property.

"My customers are all Cape workers," he explained, "And the only places I'll be able to move to already have businesses like mine — and the prices are real high, anyhow."

The Cape expansion means more than losing homes and businesses.

The old Dummitt grove and plantation, the oldest commercial orange grove in Florida, will go. So will the recreation building of the North Canaveral Chamber of Commerce which volunteer workers just built, then proudly decorated with their names.

And the Canaveral Club — a now defunct hunting and fishing hangout for Harvard graduates — will go, too.

But the people who are losing probably won't be remembered too long.

* * *

BREVARD County is jumping for joy.

Herb Johnson, circulation manager of the Titusville Star-Advocate, bought a disappointing North Merritt Island orange grove a few years ago.

Now he's going to get his money out, and, he said, "you knew me when I was a poor man."

Titusville attorney Max Brewer and banker Ed Willis, owners of substantial tracts of land in the way of the expansion, also expect to make far more than they paid for the land.

J. J. Parrish, a prominent citrus grower, and several Miami men own about 9,000 acres of cattle land near Titusville, outside the expansion, and they expect to do well with it, too.

Before the expansion announcement, they were asking $250 an acre, but you can't buy it for that now. The price is $500.

* * *

BUT, AS Mrs. Mary Edwards, a veteran Titusville real estate broker, said, it's really too early to predict the boom for Titusville — the mainland city closest to the expanded Cape.

"The Government hasn't said when it'll be paying for the land," she said, "And we don't know what the requirements will be here."

Nobody questions, though, that the boom is coming. The government has already said it'll put six new moon

rocket launching pads in the Cape — at least a 150-million-dollar job of construction alone.

And it's said it's going to shell out 50 million dollars for the land it'll take.

"I just wish though," said Mrs. Benecke, the pioneer woman, "that they'd tipped us off in advance.

"There are so many people around here getting ready to make money that there may not be any place that folks like us can afford."

"Canaveral Boom" article

109

MISCELLANOUS FAMILY PHOTOS

1st Photo: Mary Crawford Benecke holding Mary Alice Benecke. Betty Benecke Astin holding Anna Benecke. The babies are children of Dora Schnopp and John Henry Benecke.

2nd Photo: Betty Benecke Astin.

3rd Photo: Betty Astin holding Mary Alice Benecke.

4th Photo: Mary C. Benecke, Herman Benecke, Betty Astin.

1st Photo: Evelyn Briggs Smith, John Deneff, Anna Benecke Stalder Amerson, 1976

2nd Photo: June Benecke, Ray Benecke, their mother Mary Crawford Benecke and Betty Benecke Astin, July 1987

3rd Photo: Anna Amerson, Johnny Benecke, October 3, 1971.

4th Photo: Unidentified, Unidentified, Ray Benecke, June Benecke, Floyd Briggs, John Deneff, Evelyn Briggs Smith, Mary C. Benecke, Betty Benecke Astin

5th Photo: Johnny Stalder, Anna Laura Deneff (Herbst). July, 1976

6th Photo: Anna Benecke Stalder Amerson and Mary C. Benecke. July, 1976

1st Photo: Herman and Mary Benecke's home on Merritt Island.

2nd Photo: Herman Benecke

3rd Photo: Funeral of Henry Johan Benecke, 1935

4th Photo: Unidentified, Evelyn Briggs Smith, June Benecke, Floyd Briggs. July, 1976

5th Photo: Betty Betty (Astin) and her dad Herman Benecke.

Top Photo: Leslie Briggs, Charlie Stalder and John Deneff on steps of Benecke homestead, Merritt Island, Florida. 1935

Bottom Photo: *Front row* – Lena Benecke Briggs, Herman Benecke, Rose Benecke Deneff
Back row – Anna Benecke Stalder Amerson, Lillie Benecke Caudill, Laura Benecke Koleff

113

1st Photo: June Benecke in front; Wylie Slaughter in back, other men are unidentified

2nd Photo: Home of Audrey and June Benecke, Happy Creek.

3rd Photo: Wylie Slaughter, Happy Creek Hunting and Fish Camp.

Pictures of Happy Creek Hunting
and Fishing Camp 1956 – 1961

My fourth grade class on Merritt Island

Sara S. Anderson

TEACHER   4TH GRADE

MERRITT ISLAND ELEMENTARY SCHOOL
MERRITT ISLAND, FLORIDA

Ellis V. C.

PRINCIPAL

1955-1956

I was sick the day of this class picture, so I later cut out my individual picture from that year and pasted myself in! We lived on State Route 3 South in a two story house among five acres of orange groves. Each morning, I would wait upstairs watching for the bus. When it would come into view from around the bend, I would yell,

'Bus is coming!' run downstairs, out the door to the road, get on the bus and go to school. I remember watching Superman on TV in the late afternoon lying on top of the back of the couch (which I was not supposed to do) when Daddy would come home from work. As soon as I saw him through the screen door, I would quickly hop off the couch and lie on the floor as if I had been there all along!

Our home during 1955

I took this picture in 1982 and the house looks much the same today as when my family lived there.

Our Lives Now

RAY BENECKE (85) The older son of Herman Benecke, Henry Johan's son, I was born on Happy Creek, Merritt Island, Florida. I graduated from Titusville High School in 1938 and worked with my father and brother fishing on and around Merritt Island. We were commercial fishermen and operated Happy Creek Hunting and Fishing Lodge. I was drafted into the Florida National Guard in 1941, the 124th Division. June's wife introduced me to my wife, Catherine. We married in 1962 in Titusville, by family friend Judge Virgil Conklin. Catherine and I now live on the Indian River, next door to June and Audrey and have a direct view of the VAB building and watch all the launches of Kennedy Space Center. I have lived a happy and contented life and have no complaints whatsoever about any of it. I do sometimes wonder what our life would be like now, though, if the spaceport had not been built on our homeplace.

Mother: Mary Crawford Benecke
Father: Herman Benecke

DENTON STEVEN KOLEFF (84) Sadly, Denton passed away July 2, 2004 at his home in Tamarac, Florida. He grew up in Sanford, Florida, owned a filling station but sold that when he joined the Marines. Married M. Helen Yaksh in Milwaukee, Wisconsin, and worked as a Steward on oar boats on the Great Lakes until retirement. They then moved to Ft. Lauderdale, Florida.

Mother: Laura Benecke Koleff LaRoche
Father: Pete Koleff

ANNA LAURA HERBST (83) I have resided in Sanford, Florida all of my life, graduating from Sanford High School in 1939. Mother was very ill when I was in high school and this created a hardship on all of us. I married Harold E. Herbst August 21, 1942 and we had two sons, Alan and Harold, Jr. After the boys were in high school, I returned to work. I worked with R. H. Dougherty, Optometrist, retiring after 27 years. I became a member of the Sanford-Seminole Art Association in 1964, earning a 'Best

118

in Show', 'First Place' and 'Honorable Mention' for my oil and watercolor paintings. I have been a substitute teacher, a member of the Pilot Club International, taught Sunday School, and helped organize thirteen years of Swedish Supper each March at my church. Harold and I were married 55 years. He passed away in 1995. I stay active within my community and plan to take up my painting again!

Mother: Rose Benecke Deneff
Father: John Deneff

VIOLETTE CAROLYN KOLEFF GUTH (82)   I live in California with my husband, Charles Guth. We've been married since 1977. I have two grown children: A daughter, Gayle Lazur, who lives in Lynnwood, Washington; and a son, William Hunter, Jr. who lives in Easton, Maryland with his wife, Christine. They have three boys all in their thirties. I have three grandsons, one living in New Hampshire and two living in Marietta, Georgia. I have no great grandchildren yet, but keep hoping.

William Hunter and I came to California in 1947 after World War II to attend college at the University of California in Berkeley. After graduating, I worked for the Oakland Unified School System for 27 years, retiring in 1982. While employed in Oakland I was a teacher for five years and Project Coordinator for Headstart State Preschool Programs at 14 elementary school sites.

Bill Jr. graduated from the University of California, Berkeley and attended Hastings Law School in San Francisco. After graduating, he worked for the Justice Department in Washington, D.C. for five years. He left the Justice Department to start his own business. Gayle graduated from University of California at Davis, and now works as an underwriter for an insurance company. She and her husband, George, have no children.

My brother, Denton Koleff lives in Ft. Lauderdale, Florida with his wife Helen. Margarette and Herman have both passed away

Mother: Laura Benecke Koleff LaRoche
Father: Pete Koleff

JUNE BENECKE (80)   I was born at Happy Creek. I loved my surroundings, learned to hunt and fish from my father, Herman. My brother Ray and I ran Happy Creek Hunting and Fishing Lodge. It was a very large part of my life and I miss it to this day.

I met Audrey Horeicher, married and instantly had a family. Audrey has always been by my side and was very instrumental in the running of the Lodge. An accom-

plished artist, she painted my family home on Happy Creek. The palm in that picture is the only Coconut Palm on that part of the island, that we know of.

Mother: Mary Crawford Benecke
Father: Herman Benecke

Painting by Audrey Benecke of Herman and Mary Beneck's home on Merritt Island.

120

IRIS CAUDILL (80)   I started work with Constable Pat Gordon in January of 1943 and became his Deputy Constable in 1948. Mr. Gordon was defeated in his re-election run and I started working for attorney H. E. Oxford until Pat Gordon ran again and won. I worked with him for six more years. When he was elected sheriff, I was the Chief Office Deputy and was still able to serve papers. Everyone respected Mr. Gordon and because of this, I was able to serve papers in very rough areas of town. Those who did not know my real name when I tried to serve papers, called me Miss Pat! The old timers still call me that. In 1972 the Florida

Legislature abolished the Constable position, which put me out of a job. I began work for attorney Dennis Fontaine, a young lawyer in Lakeland, who was opening his private office. I worked with Dennis for 21 years.

Mother: Lillie Benecke Caudill
Father: Stuart Caudill, Sr.

EVELYN BRIGGS SMITH (78) I grew up on Merritt Island and remember well my mother (Lena) and her siblings speaking in their native tongue of German. I had a magical childhood with the ocean, rivers and lakes of North Merritt Island as my playground. We used to lie on top of the cabin launch and watch the stars at night. The sky would turn black with ducks in the spring as they migrated south. I would help Mama plant cow peas, beans, okra, corn, sweet and Irish potatoes, squash, and much more each year in our garden. I got to play occasionally at the Canaveral Lighthouse, the Coast Guard Station often as they were friends of ours, and run barefoot through the sandy beaches. I was taught how to be self-sufficient and how to live off the land.

I married in 1948 to Floyd Lane Smith and lived for a short time in Pennsylvania on my in-laws farm. We eventually moved back to Florida and built a home in the little town of Merritt on West Lucas Street. The house we lived in is still there but the area has sadly turned into much less of a rural area! We had four children: Dale Kenneth, Donald Lee (born on Leap Year 1952), Charlotte Ann and Karen Denise. Floyd and I divorced in 1961 and we sadly lost contact over the years. The last contact we had with Floyd was in 1962 and he was living in Los Angeles County, California.

I have six grandchildren: Patrick Kenneth Smith, Jason Smith, Joshua Smith, Douglas Robbins, Deanna Robbins, and Melissa Dutton. I am retired from Cape Canaveral Air Force Station where I worked as a timekeeper, climbed the tall stacks as an inventory clerk, and worked in vehicle maintenance. One of the departments I worked in involved taking care of the needs of the people who went down range. We did payroll, vehicle rentals, etc. Down range bases included the Grand Bahamas, Maui, and the Ascension Islands.

I now work part-time with Publix Supermarket, enjoy my grandchildren, garden, and am active in my church. God has blessed me with health, wonderful children and a loving family.

Mother: Lena Benecke Briggs
Father: Dorr Angelo Briggs

DAVID ZANE CAUDILL, SR. (76) I am the youngest of the four children of Lillie Elizabeth Benecke Caudill and Stuart H. Caudill, Sr. I had two older brothers, William Lewellyn Caudill and Stuart Hagard Caudill, Jr., and have one sister, Iris Caudill. My brother William died in August 1994, and Stuart passed away in November 2003.

I was raised in and have lived in or around Lakeland, Florida all my life except while serving in the United States Navy. I joined the Navy at the age of seventeen with my mother's reluctant permission and was sent to Alaska where I trained to serve as a 'frogman', the underwater demolition unit of the Navy.

I bought my first motorcycle when I got out of the service. It was on one of the motorcycle gatherings that I met my future wife, Marie Elizabeth Ballard. We were married on Christmas Day, 1949 in Mount Tabor Church, Lakeland, Florida. I have worked for the Atlantic Coastline Railroad and the Florida Freshwater Game and Fish Commission in the Glades County area. After we started a family, Marie drove a school bus for Glades County and also worked for the Department of Agriculture as a lookout on a fire tower. When my brother William and his wife retired, I purchased their lawnmower sales and repair business. Marie and I operated this business for more than 25 years. Upon our retirement, we worked with a private hunting club and camp for over five years. I worked as a hunting guide (as my mother had) and Marie was the camp cook.

122

Mother's love for the outdoors, hunting and fishing has definitely appeared in her children and grandchildren.

Marie and I have three children: David Zane Caudill, Jr.; Michael Franklin Caudill; and Patricia Ann Caudill Watson. Zane gave us three grandsons, David Zane Caudill III, Shane Michael Caudill and Logan Mathew Caudill; Mike gave us two granddaughters: Jessica Marie Caudill and Mary Caudill. Patricia gave us two granddaughters: Brittany Nichole Hollingsworth and Shadoe Alexis Yelvington. Our granddaughter Brittany gave us a great-grandson, Jayden Ryan Johnson in November, 2003.

Mother: Lillie Benecke Caudill
Father: Stuart Caudill, Sr

BETTY BENECKE ASTIN (71)   I was born at home on Happy Creek, Merritt Island, Florida. My

mother Mary always told me she sent my brother Ray to get our grandmother Tillie, but I decided to make my appearance long before he got back with her!

Graduating from Titusville High School, I finished my education at Florida State University, receiving a degree in Home Economics in 1956.

I married Sam Astin July 12, 1960 in Tampa, Florida, and we made our home in Plant City (Winter Strawberry Capital of the World) where Sam worked with his dad on Astin Farms. While his dad grew strawberries, Sam and I decided to farm and market vegetables. We have three children, Sam, III; Laura Astin Carter; and Suzanne Astin Roberts, all who live very close to us.

We have nine grandchildren, are enjoying semi-retirement and have a summer home in the north Georgia mountain community of Tiger. We are still involved in work at Astin Farms with our children. Sam has a collection of antique automobiles and farm equipment which he is proud to show off. We have been blessed with family, good friends, good health and have dearly loved our life!

Mother: Mary Crawford Benecke
Father: Herman Johan Benecke

LEE BRIGGS (69)   I am now living in Port Orange, north of the Merritt Island area, with my wife of 47 years, Betty. Growing up on the island was ideal to a certain extent. After graduating from Titusville High, I began work with Pan Am Airways as a Supply Clerk in November, 1956. I then worked my way up to management and on up to Supervisor of Logistics where I operated Critical Spares for all launch complexes at Kennedy Space Center. I was moved from Logistics to Central Control where I worked in Range Scheduling.

In the summer of 1968, I was 'handpicked' along with a number of others to work with the Air  Force, testing weather balloons. I left Pan Am Airways in 1972 and began work with TCOM, L.P./Westinghouse in January of 1973 working with blimps and aerostats. TCOM contracted with foreign governments, which enabled me and my family to travel all over the world; namely The Bahamas, Iran, Nigeria, Israel, France and Italy for extended periods of time. This gave me and my family an exceptional education and made us appreciate America, even with all her 'problems'.

God has blessed us to be able to travel and enjoy His creation. We have seen how magnificent He is and how mankind has sometimes wasted His resources. God has richly blessed my wife Betty and me with four children, nine grandchildren and three great-grandchildren. We are now enjoying the freedom that comes with retirement and have never been busier! God is good!

Mother: Lena Benecke Briggs
Father: Dorr Angelo Briggs

Epilogue

Stepping onto the sandy soil, tears immediately came to my eyes. Feeling a tugging at my heart, I knew I had to be in the right place - Happy Creek. It was silent, still, waiting. The Australian pines whispered in the breeze; an orange tree beckoned with its young, green fruit. As I walked along the shore of the creek, the remains of a boat landing came into sight. A little further down we spotted bricks lying on the ground near the water. These bricks had to be from a chimney of one of the cabins on the river! I was standing on my ancestors' land! This land is now part of the spaceport. I could feel my ancestors' strength welling up out of the ground; strength that is now a springboard for outer-space. Through the graces of NASA, my husband and I were allowed to explore part of the land which had been home-steaded by my great-grandfather in 1887.

I truly believe America needed and needs the space center. The exploration of space has had a lasting impact on all our lives. However, I have seen first hand the hurt my family suffered with the government's handling of the take-over of their land.

In 1961, a government official visited Happy Creek prior to the initial land acquisition or announcement and rented a boat from my cousin, June Benecke. The official took pictures of the building structures that were scheduled for future demolition. This government official did not tell June what his purpose was in taking the pictures, and June did not ask. The families who lived on the island should have been given notice before anyone else of what was being planned for North Merritt Island.

Because they felt the government was not offering them fair compensation, the Benecke

> ## In 1962, they were forced off their land without a settlement

brothers sued the United States Government. In 1962, they were forced off their land without a settlement, and did not receive remuneration for another five years.

By the time the news of NASA's land expansion was officially announced, real estate values had skyrocketed. The Benecke brothers were able to find only six acres of similar land for $44,000 to replace the 60 acres they owned together on Happy Creek (the camp consisted of 33 acres. June's brother Ray owned 27 adjoining acres).

Because they ran a fishing business, they had to find land on the water and chose a location on the Indian River, directly across from the Vehical Assembly Building. Although this view is a constant reminder to what they lost, they are at least close to the land they loved.

The government wanted to acquire this land at the best price they could. Some of the owners were absent and some were part time land owners. However, the full-time residents, like my cousins, should have been shown better consideration. They were not hiding in the bush; they were operating businesses, and living in well established homes. Ray and June worked hard every day of their adult lives to preserve their father's and his father's way of life. They had their hunting and fishing lodge taken away from them without adequate notice or compensation. They were not treated with the respect I feel they deserved, and were entitled to far more than the $50,000 they had to fight the government for in court ($50,000 was the cap the government had placed on lawsuits of this type).

The land NASA and the Kennedy Space Center sits on is special land to our family. The memories of this land have been preserved as a lasting legacy by the members of my family and other families. These pioneers are still able to tell us what it was like growing up and living on North Merritt Island. These memories should never be allowed to die. I have endeavored to pass our special family heritage along to future generations of all the families who lived in this area before Kennedy Space Center.

Our families lived at the birthplace of Kennedy Space Center – what a wonderful family legacy!

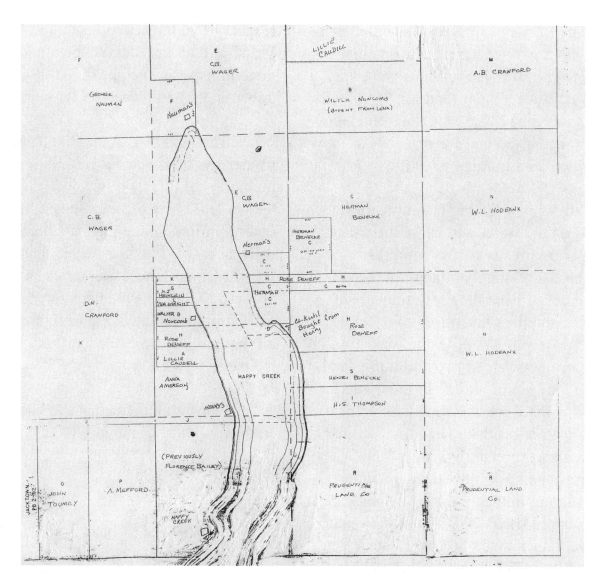

Happy Creek map showing location of land owners in 1935.

—Map courtesy of Iris Caudill

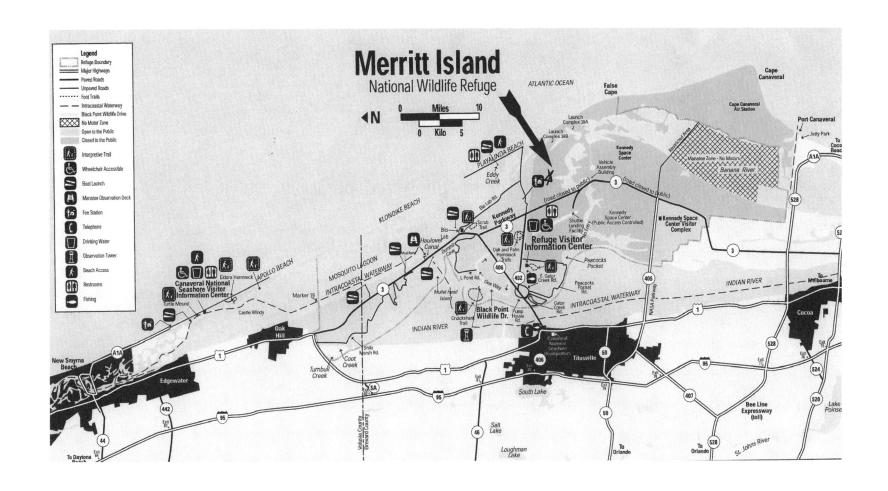

This map shows the current use of Merritt Island.
Arrow marks the Happy Creek area.

—Map courtesy of Merritt Island National Wildlife Refuge

Order Information

To order copies of this book, please write to:

Ammons Communications
29 Regal Avenue
Sylva, NC 28779

Watch for future volumns of **"Memories of Merritt Island"**

—Gail Briggs Nolen